fun Christmas crafts

to make and bake

over 60 festive projects
to make with your kids

Annie Rigg &
Catherine Woram

photography by Lisa Linder
and Polly Wreford

LONDON NEW YORK

Senior designers Toni Kay and Megan Smith
Editors Annabel Morgan and Céline Hughes
Location research Jess Walton
Picture research Emily Westlake
Production Gary Hayes
Art director Leslie Harrington
Editorial director Julia Charles
Stylists Catherine Woram and Annie Rigg

Prop stylist Liz Belton
Indexer Hilary Bird

First published in 2012
by Ryland Peters and Small

20–21 Jockey's Fields
London, WC1R 4BW
and
519 Broadway, 5th Floor
New York, NY 10012
www.rylandpeters.com

10 9 8 7 6 5 4 3 2 1

Text © Annie Rigg, Catherine Woram and Ryland
Peters & Small 2008, 2010, 2012

Design and photographs
© Ryland Peters & Small 2012

The projects and recipes in this book have been
previously published by Ryland, Peters & Small in
Christmas Crafting with Kids and *Christmas
Cooking with Kids*.

ISBN: 978-1-84597-273-2

A CIP record for this book is available
from the British Library.

US Library of Congress Cataloging-in-
publication data has been applied for.

Printed and bound in China

fun Christmas crafts

to make and bake

Contents

introduction

Christmas is the perfect time for kids to get creative. When the weather gets chilly and the mood gets festive, the projects in this book are a brilliant way to keep little hands busy getting ready for the holiday season. Whether making decorations for the tree, cards to give to friends and family, or treats for a Christmas party, there is something to interest any child, and the wide variety of fun projects will appeal to younger children as well as experienced crafters and bakers right up to the age of 10 and beyond.

Fun to Make! includes many of the traditional crafting techniques — from sewing a gorgeous shaker-style stocking to using paper-cutting techniques to make decorative snowflakes and lanterns. Kids can have fun modelling and painting clay tree decorations, or using potato printing to create fun wrapping paper and cards. Let your kids go wild exploring their creativity and adding their own personal embellishments to the finished items!

Fun to Bake! will show you that Christmas is also the perfect time to get kids interested in food and cooking. Steeped in tradition and distinctive flavours, there is nothing quite like cooking up a bûche de Noël or a gingerbread house. Simple treats such as peppermint creams or coconut ice are perfect for younger children to make, and, packaged prettily in homemade gift boxes and bags, make great gifts, too. Recipes for baked treats are ideal for older children and include an easy fruitcake and iced Christmas tree cookies they can decorate using all manner of festive sprinkles and edible sparkles.

This year, make your family Christmas a homemade one with these enjoyable, creative projects that are sure to have grown-ups rolling up their sleeves and joining in the fun, too!

Fun to Make!

decorations

pompom tree decorations

Pompoms are fun and easy to make, and you can use them to create cute Christmas tree baubles. Alternatively, you could make two different-sized pompoms and glue them together to make a snowman or robin, or even a Father Christmas figure complete with felt hat!

You will need:
paper • pencil • cardboard
• scissors • assorted balls of
wool • 3-D fabric pen in red
• approx 10cm/4in gingham
ribbon per bauble

wind the wool   Trace the disc template on page 154 onto paper and cut it out. Place it on a piece of cardboard and draw round it. Repeat. Cut out the two discs. Cut a length of wool about 2m/2yd long and wind into a small ball that will fit through the hole in the discs. Start to wind wool around the discs, binding them together. When the ball of wool is finished, tie the end to the beginning of a new one. Continue to wind wool round the discs until they are completely covered.

cut around the outside   When the winding process is complete, hold the pompom discs securely and cut around the edges of the wool using scissors. The wool will fall away from the disc and look like fringing at this point. It is important that the two discs are firmly held together.

secure the wool   Cut two lengths of wool about 20cm/8in long and thread between the two cardboard discs. Pull them together tightly and knot tightly. The loose ends of this wool will form the hanging loop for the decoration, so tie another knot about 8cm/3in from the first knot and neatly trim the ends.

finish off   Gently pull the cardboard discs away from the pompom. If it proves difficult, just cut them off. Trim any excess bits of wool, and fluff the pompom to give it a nice round shape. Use a 3-D fabric pen to draw tiny dots on the pompom and finish with a length of red gingham ribbon tied in a bow around the hanging loop.

snowmen

Make one small and one large pompom using white wool and tie the two together using the wool ends. Trim any uneven ends. Now tie a green pipe cleaner around the snowman's neck to create a scarf, and twist a black pipe cleaner into a hat shape. Glue on a triangle of orange felt for a carrot nose, and use a 3-D fabric pen to draw on his eyes and buttons.

robin tree decoration

Make a small pompom in brown wool for the head. Now wind brown wool around one half of two larger pompom discs and red wool around the other half. Snip around the edges of the disc and secure the pompom with a length of wool. Use the wool ends to tie the two pompoms together to form a robin. Add a triangle of red felt for his beak and bend brown pipe cleaners into shape for his feet.

father christmas

Make one large pompom from red wool for the body. To make the head, wind red wool around one half of two smaller pompom discs and white wool around the other half. Snip around the edges of the disc and secure the pompom with a length of wool. Use the wool ends to tie the two pompoms together to form a cuddly Father Christmas figure. Add a hat formed from a quarter-circle of red felt, and a black felt belt. Use a black 3-D fabric pen to draw on his eyes and buttons.

little tips
Remember: the more wool you manage to wind around the discs, the fatter your pompom will be.
For a really plump pompom, try winding the wool around the discs twice.

cinnamon sticks

A bundle of cinnamon sticks tied together with red gingham ribbon and finished with a tiny jingle bell makes a pretty and fragrant addition to any Christmas tree.

**You will need
(for each decoration):**
five cinnamon sticks • scissors
• 40cm/16in red gingham
ribbon (7mm/⅜in wide) •
5cm/2in thin wire • small
gold bell

bundle cinnamon together

Cut a 20cm/8in length of gingham ribbon.
Lay it flat on a table and place the five
cinnamon sticks on top. Wind the ribbon
around the sticks once and pull the ends
of the ribbon tight.

arrange ribbon on sticks
Take the remaining
piece of ribbon and lay it on top of the cinnamon sticks,
running in the same direction as them, so that the ribbon
forms the shape of a cross.

make hanging loop
Bring the two ends of the first piece of ribbon up
from beneath the cinnamon sticks, and knot them on top of the sticks. Now
make another knot approx 5cm/2in further up the ribbon. This will form a loop
to hang the decoration from.

finish off
Tie the ends of the second
piece of ribbon into a neat bow. Now
thread the jingle bell onto the piece of wire,
and push the wire through the knot of the
bow. Twist the ends of the wire together to
secure the bell in place, and trim the wire
ends to finish.

You will need:
square pieces of paper •
pencil • scissors

fold paper Take a square piece of paper. Fold it in half diagonally to form a triangle. Then fold in half again and then into quarters. You should now have a small folded triangle shape.

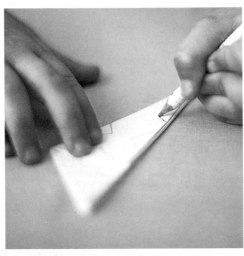

draw on design Using the pencil, draw triangular or scalloped shapes on the folded edges of the paper. You can draw curved shapes on the top edges of the paper (furthest from the centre of the paper), too. Experiment with different shapes, so that all your snowflakes are slightly different.

cut out Using scissors, carefully cut along the lines you have drawn on the paper. The more shapes you cut out, the more decorative and delicate the finished snowflake will be.

pull open Gently unfold the paper and carefully press it flat to reveal the snowflake's design. You can cut snowflakes from any piece of paper, but good sizes are a 20cm/8in square for a large snowflake and a 10cm/4in square for a small one.

paper snowflakes

Paper snowflakes are so simple to make, yet so effective. Snip them from white paper, tissue paper or tracing paper to create pretty and inexpensive Christmas decorations. They can be used to decorate windows or suspended from lengths of cotton for a mobile effect. Alternatively, use them to adorn a vase of bare branches to make a striking tabletop display.

18 fun to make!

You will need:
**fresh oranges • sharp knife •
dish towel • paper towels
• baking sheet • wooden
skewer • 15cm/6in gingham
ribbon (10mm/½in wide) for
each hanging loop**

slice the oranges   Ask an adult to cut the orange slices approximately 5mm/¼in wide. Lay the slices on the dish towel and blot them with paper towels to remove any excess moisture. This will speed up the drying process.

bake in oven   Lay the orange slices on the baking sheet. Put them in the oven on the very lowest setting and leave them for about four hours or until they are completely dry. The trick is to let them 'cook' long enough to dry completely. If they do not dry entirely, they won't keep for long and may go mouldy. Ask an adult to remove the baking sheet from the oven, as it will be very hot.

remove dried oranges   Once the baking sheet has completely cooled, remove the orange slices from the sheet and set them aside for decorating. The slices should be hard and dry, but retain their citrussy fragrance.

finish off   Ask an adult to make a small hole in the orange using a sharp point such as a wooden skewer. Thread the ribbon through the hole and tie the ends in a knot. Trim the ribbon ends on the diagonal to prevent them from fraying.

orange tree decorations

*Dried orange slices hung from a ribbon loop
make fragrant and unusual tree decorations.*

mini tree

Use a real or artificial miniature tree to create a fun and festive centrepiece for the Christmas table. Kids will enjoy decorating it with tiny baubles, miniature pompoms and candy canes made from twisted pipe cleaners.

You will need:
miniature Christmas tree • terracotta pot
• paintbrushes • undercoat • silver paint •
1m/1yd gingham ribbon (2.5cm/1in wide) •
scissors • glue • red and white pipe cleaners
• 1m silver ribbon (5mm/¼in wide) • red and
silver miniature pompoms • 2m/2yd gingham
ribbon (1cm/½in) wide • miniature baubles
(if desired)

paint pot   Apply a layer of undercoat to the terracotta pot and
let it dry completely. Now apply a coat of silver paint and let dry.
If necessary, apply a second coat of silver paint for more even
coverage, and let it dry.

attach ribbon and bow   Measure the circumference of the
top of the pot and cut a length of the wider gingham ribbon to fit.
Glue it around the rim of the pot. Tie a neat bow from the same
ribbon and glue it to the front of the pot. Let the glue dry.

make candy canes   Twist the bottom ends of the pipe
cleaners together so they are attached. Now wind them
together for a striped effect.

shape canes   Carefully bend one end
of the twisted pipe cleaners to form a
candy-cane shape with a curved top.
Now they can simply be hooked onto
the Christmas tree.

make hanging loop Cut a 6cm/2½in length of the narrow silver ribbon. Fold it in half and pinch the ends together to form a loop. Apply a small dab of glue to hold the ends in place. Let the glue dry.

attach loop Using a pair of scissors, carefully snip open a pompom so that you can see the centre. Apply a dab of glue to the middle of the pompom and push in the end of the loop. Press the two sides of the opening closed. Allow the glue to dry completely before hanging the pompoms from the tree.

tie on bows Cut lengths of the narrower gingham ribbon and tie them into bows on the ends of the branches of the Christmas tree. Cut the ends of ribbon on the diagonal to prevent them from fraying.

tie tree topper Cut a 20cm/8in length of the wider gingham ribbon and tie it around the top of the Christmas tree to make a tree topper. Cut the ends on the diagonal to prevent the ribbon fraying.

little tips
The red colour scheme we used would work equally well in golds and silvers to create a more luxurious feel for a Christmas table. Or try using all white for an icy winter theme.

24 fun to make!

You will need:
decorative wrapping paper •
scissors • pencil • ruler • glue
• sequin trim to decorate
(20cm/8in per lantern)

cut and fold paper Cut a square
of wrapping paper measuring 20cm/8in
by 20cm/8in for the lantern and a strip
of paper 1.5cm/¾in by 20cm/8in for the
handle to hang it from. Fold the square
of paper in half and press flat.

snip lantern holes Take the piece of folded paper and,
cutting inwards from the folded edge of the paper, use scissors
to snip flaps that finish about 3cm/1¼in from the top of the paper.
Each flap should be spaced about 2cm/¾in apart. You may want
to mark out the lines using a pencil and a ruler first, to make it
easier to cut the paper properly.

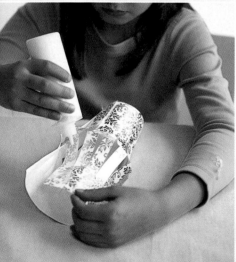

glue into round To make the lantern shape, unfold the paper and roll it to
form a tube shape with the paper slits running vertically. Glue the edges of the
paper together to form a round tubular lantern, then press downwards gently
to form a splayed lantern shape.

finish off Cut a piece of sequin trim to fit
around the top of the lantern and glue it in
place. Glue the ends of the hanging loop to
the inside of the lantern on both sides and
let dry completely.

paper lanterns

Paper lanterns are a traditional and fun way of using a piece of paper to make three-dimensional objects. They look very pretty fashioned from soft pink and silver wrapping paper and trimmed with sequins for a festive look. They would also look great in simple red and white trimmed with patterned ribbon.

snow globes

Snow globes make great gifts for friends and family, and children really enjoy making them.

You will need:

empty, clean jam jars with lids
• silver paint • paintbrush
• strong waterproof glue
or tile adhesive • Christmas
decorations to put in jar •
jug/pitcher and spoon for
pouring • distilled water •
glycerine • clear washing-up
liquid/detergent • glitter

paint lid   Paint the lid of the jam jar with silver paint and let it dry completely. You may wish to sand the metal lid lightly before painting so the paint adheres better to the surface. If required, apply a second coat of paint for better coverage and again leave to dry.

attach decoration   Use strong glue to firmly attach the decoration to the inside of the jam jar lid. If the decoration is on the small side, build up a small mound using waterproof tile adhesive and press the decoration firmly into this. Leave until completely dry.

fill jar and add glitter   Use a jug/pitcher to pour the distilled water into the jam jar. Fill it right up to the brim. Now stir in two teaspoons of glycerine and half a teaspoon of washing-up liquid. Add five or six spoonfuls of glitter to the water. White or silver glitter looks most similar to snow, although bright colours like red or green can look very jolly and festive.

finish off   Carefully place the lid on the top of the jam jar and screw the lid tightly in place. The jam jar should be watertight, but you may wish to seal it around the edges with a thin layer of silicone sealant, which is available from good craft stores.

christmas stocking

Create this pretty Shaker-style stocking in cream wool and decorate with a simple heart and mother-of-pearl button. You could make one for each member of the family and tie on card name tags.

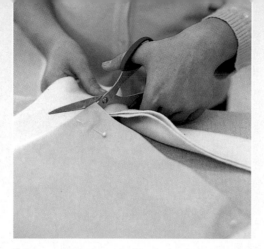

You will need:
paper • pencil • scissors • 40cm/16in cream
wool fabric (137cm/44in wide) • pins • red
felt for heart motif (15cm x 15cm/6in x 6in)
• needle • white thread • red thread • glue
• pearl button • red embroidery thread •
20cm/8in gingham fabric (137cm/44in wide)
• 10cm/4in gingham ribbon

create a template   Trace the stocking template on page 155 onto
a piece of paper. Now enlarge it on a photocopier at 200% to make it
the right size. Cut out the template. Fold the cream wool fabric in half
and pin the template to the fabric. Cut out the stocking pieces.

cut out heart motif   Trace the heart template on page
155 onto a piece of paper and cut it out. Pin the template
to the red felt and cut out a heart to decorate the front of
the stocking.

tack heart to stocking   Thread the needle
with white cotton and tack the heart motif to the
front stocking piece.

blanket-stitch heart   Now thread
the needle with red cotton and work
small blanket stitches all the way around
the heart motif. When you have finished,
remove the tacking. Now use a dab of
glue to stick the pearl button to the
centre of the heart.

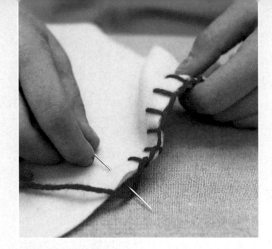

stitch stocking together

With right sides facing, tack the two stocking pieces together. Turn right side out. Thread a needle with the red embroidery thread and work blanket stitch all the way around the edges of the stocking, leaving the straight top edges of the stocking open. Press flat using a warm iron (it is advisable for an adult to do this).

make gingham border

Take the piece of gingham fabric. Fold it in half lengthways, right sides together, and stitch the side seams together using small running stitches. Turn right side out and press flat using an iron (it is advisable for an adult to do this).

stitch gingham to stocking

Turn a 1cm/½in hem to the inside of the gingham and press flat. Tuck about 8cm/3in of the gingham fabric inside the stocking and fold the remainder of the fabric over the top of the stocking, with the hemmed edge on the outside. Sew small running stitches all around the top of the gingham fabric to hold it in place.

sew on hanging loop

Fold the piece of gingham ribbon in half to form a loop, and stitch it to the inside of the gingham fabric at the back seam of the stocking.

little tips
The stocking would work equally well in a bright Christmassy red colour. Other jolly variations would be a star or Christmas tree motif on the front of the stocking. Alternatively, you could write on your name using a 3-D fabric pen.

angel tree topper

Decorate simple cones of card with a sprinkling of glitter and a pompom to create pretty tree-top angels complete with silver pipe cleaner or feather wings.

You will need:
25cm/10in diameter plate as template for cone shape • silver card • pencil • scissors • glue • silver glitter • stapler • silver pipe cleaner • pompom for head • blue and pink 3-D fabric pens for face • gold pipe cleaner

draw around plate   Place the plate on the silver card and draw around half of it to create a semi-circle for the cone. Cut out.

apply glitter   Use glue to draw a scalloped line all around the curved edge of the semi-circular piece of card. Sprinkle silver glitter over the glue and leave for a few minutes. Shake off any excess glitter and allow the glue to dry completely.

form cone shape   Form the card semi-circle into a cone shape (folding it gently in half and making a slight crease at the centre of the card makes it a bit easier to form a cone). Use a stapler to join the card together.

make wings   Use the silver pipe cleaner to form the wings. Twist the ends over to form a figure of eight.

attach wings   Apply a dab of glue to the centre of the wings and glue them to the back of the cone, about 3cm/1¼in down from the top. Allow glue to dry completely.

glue on pompom head   Use a ready-made pompom or make your own following the instructions on pages 10–11. Glue the pompom to the top of the cone and leave to dry.

draw face   Use 3-D fabric pens in pink and blue to draw the angel's eyes and mouth on the pompom. Leave to dry.

finish off   For a halo, bend a gold pipe cleaner into a circular shape with a diameter of about 3cm/1¼in. Twist the ends together to secure, and glue it to the top of the pompom head to finish.

little tips
Use red card to make a Santa Claus tree topper complete with a cotton-wool beard or a Rudolf the reindeer tree topper using brown card and a pair of pipe-cleaner antlers!

paperchains

Traditional paperchains are easy to make and look great made in festive paper for Christmas. We used decorative gold and silver patterned wrapping paper, but they would work equally well in red and white or even icy blues and silver tones.

You will need:
scissors • gold and silver wrapping paper • pencil • ruler • glue • stapler (if desired)

draw lines on paper Cut the wrapping paper into pieces that are at least 20cm/8in long. Using a pencil and ruler, draw lines on the back of the paper, making sure that each one is approximately 2cm/¾in wide. Repeat with the different coloured paper.

cut out strips   Use the scissors to cut out the paper strips. It is a good idea to keep the colours separate by making a pile of strips in each colour, so they are easier to select when making the chain.

form first link Bend the paper to form a loop and apply a dab of glue to fix it together. Press flat and allow glue to dry. You can use a stapler instead of glue, which is quicker, but the staples will be visible.

continue making chain
Thread the end of a second paper strip through the first loop and glue the ends together. Continue threading alternate strips of silver and gold paper until you have made the required length of paperchain.

You will need:
air-drying modelling clay •
rolling pin • snowflake-shaped
cookie cutter • drinking straw
(for piercing hole) • spatula
• paints in desired colours •
saucer for paint • paintbrushes
• glue • glitter • ribbon for
hanging loop (5mm/¼in wide)

roll out clay   Remove the clay from its packaging and knead to soften it. Roll the clay out with a rolling pin. For smaller snowflakes, the clay should be about 5mm thick. For larger snowflakes, the clay should be about 8mm/⅓in thick.

cut out shape   Use the snowflake cookie cutter to cut the shape from the clay. Carefully remove the excess clay from around the cutter before lifting it off. Use the end of a drinking straw to pierce a ribbon hole to hang the snowflake from. Use a spatula to lift the clay shape and place it on a tray to dry. When the top is dry, turn the shape over so the other side can dry completely, too. This prevents the edges from curling as the clay dries.

paint and decorate   Apply a coat of white paint to the top and sides of each snowflake and allow to dry completely. When dry, paint the other side. Leave to dry. If necessary, apply a further coat of paint for better coverage.

finish off   Apply dots of glue to the front of the decoration and then sprinkle silver glitter over the snowflake. Gently shake off the glitter onto a plate, and leave to dry. Cut an 8cm/3in length of ribbon and thread it through the hole in the snowflake. Knot the ends of the ribbon to form a hanging loop for the decoration.

clay decorations

Children love working with clay, and it can be used to create fun festive-shaped decorations that are then painted and decorated with glitter, and threaded onto ribbon to hang from the tree. Other Christmassy cookie cutters can be used to make more decorations such as stockings or bells, as shown on page 7.

little tips
Avoid putting the clay near water, as it will make it sticky and difficult to use. Keep any left-over clay wrapped in plastic in an airtight container for future use. A couple of coats of water-based varnish (applied by an adult) will give the painted clay a longer life.

hanging felt stars

Cut from red and green felt using pinking shears, these jolly tree decorations are an ideal easy sewing project for little fingers. We decorated the star shapes with pretty buttons and hung them from ricrac braid loops.

You will need:

paper • pencil • scissors •
coloured felt • pins • pinking
shears • 15cm/6in red ricrac per
decoration • matching cotton
thread • needle • polyester
stuffing • glue • assorted
pearl buttons (approx 8 per
decoration)

make template   Trace the star
template on page 154 onto paper
and cut it out.

draw around template   Fold the felt in half, as you
will need two star shapes per decoration. Use a pencil to draw
around the star motif on the felt fabric (it may be easier if you
first pin the star motif to the felt to keep it in place).

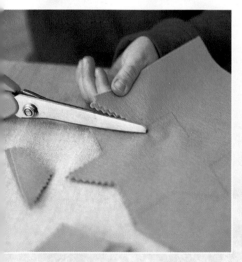

cut out   Using pinking shears, carefully cut all the way around the star shape, making
sure you are cutting through both layers of fabric. The pinking shears give an attractive
zigzag effect to the edges and, if you are using cotton or linen, will prevent the fabric
from fraying. If you are making more than one star decoration, it is a good idea to cut
them all out at one time.

attach loop   Fold a 15cm/6in length of
ricrac braid in half and place between the
two layers of felt at the top of one of the
points. Thread the needle. Push the needle
through the two layers of felt, sandwiching
the loop between them, and make two or
three stitches to secure the hanging loop.

little tips
Use different shapes such as hearts and fill with dried lavender
to make cute scented gifts for your family and friends. Sequins
or beads can be used instead of buttons for a more festive look.

stitch together   Continue stitching all the way around the points of the star, using small running stitches about 3mm/¼in from the edge. Stitch around five sides of the star but leave the sixth side open so you can add the stuffing.

stuff heart   Carefully push the stuffing into the opening. You may need to use the end of a knitting needle or a pencil to make sure that the stuffing is pushing right into all the points of the star.

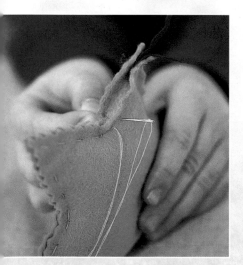

stitch opening closed   Hold the two layers of felt together and stitch the opening closed, using the same small running stitches about 3mm/¼in from the edges of the fabric. Cast off the stitching by making two or three stitches together, and snip the loose ends of the cotton.

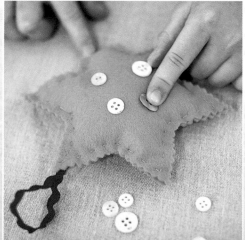

finish off   Use dabs of glue to stick the buttons to the front of the star decoration and leave to dry completely. You may wish to glue buttons to the other side of the decoration if they are to be hung on a tree, and you will need extra buttons for this.

christmas crackers

Making your own crackers is fun and easy, and it means you can put your own choice of novelties and silly handwritten jokes inside. Make the crackers from colourful wrapping paper and trim them with sequins or glitter finished with pretty bows.

You will need:

cardboard toilet rolls • 20cm x 30cm/8in x 8in piece of paper per cracker • pencil • ruler • scissors • glue or sticky tape • snaps for cracker • gifts, paper hats and jokes • 20cm/8in ribbon (5mm/¼in wide) per cracker • sequin trim

mark paper Lay the cardboard roll in the centre of the paper and mark the position of each end using a pencil. Set the roll aside.

draw lines Using the marks made on the paper as a guide, fold the paper in, right sides together, and press the folds flat. Using a ruler, mark out lines along the paper about 1.5cm/⅜in apart, starting about 2.5cm/1in in from the outside edge of the paper.

cut slits Use scissors to cut along the marked lines to create slits in the paper. Repeat on the other side. These slits enable the cracker ends to be tied more easily.

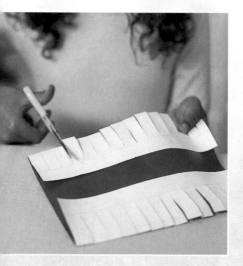

roll cracker Now unfold the paper and lay it flat. Place the cardboard roll on top. Apply a dab of glue or use a small piece of sticky tape to hold the paper on the roll. Wrap the paper around the roll as tightly as you can.

glue paper to roll Apply glue along the whole edge of the paper and press firmly in place. Allow to dry completely.

insert snap Push the cracker snap through the open end of the roll. This is also the time to insert any small gifts or trinkets, a paper hat, and a joke or other motto.

tie on ribbon Tie a 10cm/4in length of ribbon around one end of the cracker. Tie in a knot. Repeat at the other end. Trim the ends of the ribbon on the diagonal with scissors, to prevent them fraying.

finish off Measure the circumference of the cracker and cut three lengths of sequin trim to fit. Glue the sequin trim in rows around the cracker. Allow glue to dry completely.

little tips
Crackers are also a novel way of
wrapping smaller gifts – pop the gift in
with the cracker snap, then tie a pretty
matching gift tag to one end of the
cracker to finish.

twiggy wreath

Make this decorative door wreath from natural twigs
and decorate with dried leaves painted silver and gold.
Hang it on the front door, or lay it flat on a table and fill
the centre with candles for a striking table decoration.

You will need:
assortment of natural-coloured twigs • 25cm/10in diameter florist's wire ring • string • scissors • dried leaves in assorted shapes • gold and silver paint • paintbrush • glue • 50cm/18in gold ribbon (3cm/1¼in wide) for bow

tie on twigs   Carefully bend the twigs in place around the wire ring and use short lengths of string to tie them in place. Continue until the wire ring is completely covered with and concealed by the twigs. Trim any very long twigs with scissors.

paint leaves   Lay the dried leaves facing upwards on a large piece of paper and paint each one with gold or silver paint. Let them dry thoroughly and apply a further coat to each leaf if better coverage is required.

glue on leaves   Apply three or four dabs of glue to the back of a leaf and stick it to the twigs. Continue to glue on the leaves, placing them at regular intervals and alternating between silver and gold, until the wreath is covered with a layer of painted leaves.

finish off   Tie the length of gold ribbon at the top of the wreath and make a bow. Trim the ends of the ribbon on the diagonal to prevent them from fraying.

candle centrepiece

A simple terracotta flowerpot painted silver, decorated with ivy leaves and holding a simple pillar candle makes a simple yet effective centrepiece for the Christmas table. Group them together in a row of three for a more dramatic effect.

You will need:
terracotta flowerpot (15cm/6in diameter) • undercoat • silver paint • paintbrushes • double-sided sticky tape • 50cm/18in sheer silver ribbon (2.5cm/1in wide) • pillar candle (approx 20cm/8in tall) • sand or fine gravel • fresh or artificial ivy leaves

paint flowerpot Apply a coat of undercoat to the terracotta pot and leave to dry completely. Now apply a coat of silver paint and let dry. Paint the inside of the pot and leave to dry. If necessary, apply a further coat of paint for better coverage, then allow to dry completely.

tie on bow Place a small piece of double-sided sticky tape at the back of the pot on the rim and press the centre of the ribbon onto this so it is securely fixed in place. Tie the ribbon into a decorative bow at the front of the pot. Trim the ends of the ribbon on the diagonal to prevent the ends from fraying.

add candle Place the candle in the terracotta pot. If it is slightly wobbly, you may find it easier to put some sand or fine gravel in the bottom of the pot to support the candle and hold it in place. Remember to cover the hole in the base of the pot with a piece of sticky tape first!

finish off Use fresh or artificial ivy leaves to decorate around the rim of the pot. You will need to use a dab of glue to hold them in place. If the pot is intended as a gift, it is better to use artificial leaves, as they will last longer.

orange pomanders

These traditional pomanders made from oranges and decorated with cloves have long been associated with Christmas. Their sweet, spicy smell makes them welcome gifts for family and friends, or pretty decorations to hang in the home.

You will need:
ballpoint pen • large orange
• bradawl (for piercing holes)
• cloves • 60cm/15in ribbon
(1cm/½in wide) • scissors • pin

mark ribbon positions Use the ballpoint pen to mark out the position of the ribbon around the orange. The ribbon is wrapped round the orange in the shape of a cross. Use the bradawl to pierce holes for the cloves on the four quarters of the orange. Bradawls are very sharp, so it is advisable for an adult to pierce the holes.

insert cloves Carefully push the cloves into the orange. The tops of the cloves tend to be quite brittle, so push them in gently. Continue to push the cloves into the orange until all four quarters are covered.

fix ribbon Wrap a length of ribbon around the orange so the ends overlap at the bottom of the orange. Snip the ribbon and hold the first piece in place as you wrap another length around the orange. Trim any trailing ribbon ends. Now push a pin through the ends of the ribbon to hold it in place.

finish off Thread a length of ribbon through the top of the crossed ribbon on the orange and tie the ends together. Tie a knot in the ribbon about 5cm/2in from the top of the orange to form a loop. Now thread a further length of ribbon through the top of the ribbon and tie into a pretty bow to finish.

cards & wrapping

3-D christmas cards

*Simple yet effective, these gorgeous 3-D cards can be made
using scraps of decorative wallpaper or offcuts of wrapping
paper cut into festive shapes then glued to plain cards.*

You will need:
paper • pencil • scissors
• blank cards • scraps of
wallpaper or decorative
wrapping paper for motifs
• pinking shears • glue

create template Trace the star template on page 154 onto a piece of plain paper and cut it out. Place the template on the back of the decorative paper, and draw around it. You will need two paper shapes per card.

cut out motifs Use the pinking shears to carefully cut out the star motifs (you could use other decorative-edged scissors for different effects). See overleaf for more ideas for different festive motifs.

make centre fold Take one of the paper star motifs and fold in half, with the right side of the paper facing inwards. Press down this fold. This is the 3-D element of the star on the front of the card.

finish off Glue the unfolded star to the front of the card, making sure that all the corners are firmly stuck down. Now dab glue all the way down the fold on the back of the second star, and stick it on top of the first star. When the glue is dry, gently fold the corners outwards to create a 3-D effect.

gold and silver hearts

Use the heart template on page 154 to cut out small and medium-sized hearts from metallic wrapping paper, using pinking shears for a decorative effect. Glue the hearts onto gold and silver cards and finish them off with dainty bows made from gold ribbon.

blue bells

Simple bell shapes cut from blue and white paper (using the template on page 154) create a pretty, punchy effect on plain white cards. They are topped with sheer white and blue ribbon bows to finish.

glittery trees

Use the template on page 155 to snip Christmas tree shapes from pretty sugar-pink and silver patterned wrapping paper. The trees are finished off with sparkling 'baubles' – pale pink and silver sequins glued to the ends of the branches.

little tips
Instead of buying whole sheets of wrapping paper, visit a craft shop and buy a pack of craft paper. These packs include an assortment of decorative printed and embroidered papers that are the perfect size for making the cards here. Scraps of wallpaper also work well, as they are thicker than wrapping paper, which makes them ideal for 3-D shapes.

You will need:
medium-sized potato •
star-shaped cookie cutter •
chopping board • sharp knife
(to be used by an adult only)
• paper towels or a dry cloth •
paints in your chosen colours
• saucers to hold the paints •
sponge paint roller • plain
white paper

cut out shape   Cut the potato in half, making sure the surface of the potato is as flat as possible. Place the cookie cutter on a chopping board with the sharp edge facing upwards. Press the potato firmly down onto the cutter, leaving the cookie cutter standing proud of the cut surface of the potato by about 5mm/¼in, so you can cut around it.

cut away edges   Ask an adult to cut away the edges of the potato using a sharp knife. This needs to be done very carefully, to ensure the star shape is as clear as possible. Press the potato down onto a dry cloth or some paper towels to remove any excess moisture, which can make the paint watery.

apply paint   Pour the paint into a saucer and use the end of the sponge paint roller to apply the paint to the star shape. Don't apply too much paint to the potato, as this will make the design bleed. If you have applied too much paint, gently blot the potato on a paper towel to remove the excess.

get printing   Begin printing. To make sure the design prints clearly, use a gentle rocking motion, moving the potato from side to side without lifting it from the paper. This will apply the paint evenly, even if the cut surface of the potato is not flat. Continue to print the stars at evenly spaced intervals. Allow the paint to dry completely.

potato print wrapping paper

Potato printing is a traditional painting technique that is a favourite with kids of all ages. They can use cookie cutters to create pretty shapes, or an adult could use a sharp knife to cut out different shapes by hand.

stamped gift bag

Use a large potato and a tree-shaped cookie cutter to decorate a paper bag and a matching gift tag to match. We used blobs of glue sprinkled with silver glitter to create the silver bauble effect on the trees and the pretty border along the top edge of the bag.

holly cards

A holly-shaped cookie cutter was used to create this festive design. It was then stamped onto plain brightly coloured pieces of card to create funky Christmas cards. Decorated with blobs of glue and a sprinkling of silver glitter, the end result looks both fun and festive.

little tips
Potato printing also looks very effective when carried out on fabric – but make sure you use fabric or stencil paint so the item can be washed. Follow the manufacturer's instructions to 'fix' the fabric paint, as some fabric paints must be fixed with a hot iron.

stamped gift tags

These pretty gift tags are made using rubber stamps featuring decorative designs. You can make your own tags using plain card, a hole punch and string ties. The stamped designs work equally well on gift cards and wrapping paper.

You will need:

card for tag • scissors • foam pad • stamping ink • rubber stamp • glue • hole punch • plain white paper • 15cm/6in string per tag

cut out gift tag Cut out a rectangle of card measuring about 8cm/3in by 15cm/6in. Use scissors to snip off the top two corners of the card on the diagonal, to form the top of the gift tag.

apply printing ink Cut out small pieces of white paper measuring about 5cm/2in by 8cm/3in. Using the foam pad, apply some stamping ink to the front of the stamp, making sure the design is completely and evenly covered.

stamp motif Place the stamp firmly on the centre of a piece of white paper and use a gentle rocking motion to make sure that the design is completely transferred onto the paper. Leave to dry completely.

finish off Glue the paper design to the front of the tag. Use a hole punch to make a hole between the two angled corners of the tag. Thread the string through the hole in the tag to finish.

You will need:
plain cake or cookie tin • red paint • paintbrush • assorted scraps of wrapping paper • scissors • glue • acrylic varnish (if desired)

paint tin   Paint the tin inside and out using the red paint, then leave it to dry. If necessary, apply a further coat of paint for better coverage, then allow the tin to dry completely.

cut paper pieces   Cut the wrapping paper into small squares and shapes using the designs of the paper as a guide. Experiment by laying out the shapes on the top of the tin lid so you can work out how many pieces of paper you will need.

découpage lid   Start by sticking the pieces of paper to the corner of the lid. If the corners of the lid are curved, you will need to cut curved corners with scissors to fit. Continue to stick pieces of the paper all over the lid until the painted area is completely covered. Once the lid is finished, leave to dry completely.

finish off   When you have finished the lid, start sticking smaller motifs such as Christmas trees all the way around the sides of the tin. Leave the tin to dry completely. You may wish to apply a couple of coats of acrylic varnish to the tin to make it more hard-wearing. Allow to dry completely.

découpaged tin

*Scraps of decorative wrapping paper glued to a plain tin
create a fantastic presentation box for home-baked gifts
such as cakes, cookies or brownies. Yum!*

You will need:
wire for hearts (30cm/12in per heart) • glass rocaille beads • pliers (if required) • silver ribbon (5mm/¼in wide) • scissors

thread beads on wire Fold the wire in half and bend it into a 'V' shape to form the base of the heart. Begin threading beads onto both sides of the wire. Continue threading until all the wire is covered, only leaving about 2cm/¾in of bare wire at each end.

shape into heart Hold the ends of the wire and bend them inwards to form the curved top of the heart. Twist the ends together to prevent the beads from falling off the wire.

twist ends of wire Twist the ends of the wire to form a loop for the ribbon. If the wire is very stiff, it may be advisable for an adult to do this, using a pair of pliers.

attach hanging loop and bow Cut a 10cm/4in length of ribbon. Thread it through the wire and knot the ends of the ribbon to form a loop. Trim the ends of the ribbon on the diagonal to prevent them fraying. Cut another length of ribbon about 10cm/4in in length and tie around the wire in a pretty bow to finish.

beaded decorations

These dainty decorations are fashioned from fine wire threaded with tiny glass rocaille beads and bent into the shape of a heart. They are perfect for adding a touch of sparkle to gifts and could also be used as Christmas tree decorations.

You will need:
round cookie cutter • felt
squares • pencil • scissors
• 15cm/6in gingham ribbon
(6mm/¼in wide) • glue •
blank cards

cut out felt motif Use the circular cookie cutter (or a similar object) as a template for the bauble shape on this card. Place it on the felt and draw round it with a pencil. Carefully cut out the bauble shape. If you are making more than one card, it's a good idea to cut out all your felt shapes at the same time.

glue on hanging loop Cut a piece of gingham ribbon about 5cm/2in long and fold it into a loop. Glue the ribbon onto the card just below where the top of the bauble will be positioned. Press down firmly to secure it in place.

stick on felt shape Apply a thin layer of glue to the back of the felt bauble shape and stick it onto the card, making sure that you have covered both the ends of the ribbon loop. Press down firmly and allow to dry completely.

finish off Make a ribbon bow from the gingham ribbon. Apply a small dab of glue to the back of the bow, and stick it to the top of the bauble, where the ribbon loop joins the bauble. Press down firmly to secure it in place and leave to dry completely.

felt motif cards

Felt is great for decorating cards, as it comes in a huge range of colours and does not fray once it is cut. We used Christmas-themed cookie cutters as templates for a variety of festive designs. Glue the felt shapes onto stiff card and finish them off with dainty ribbon bows.

christmas trees

Christmas tree cookie cutters were used to cut out these shapes from plain red, white and lime green felt. They were glued to cards, then decorated with tiny dots made using 3-D fabric pens.

glitter stars

Stars in plain and patterned felt adorn these square Christmas cards. We added a scattering of silver glitter glue dots to make the stars truly twinkle.

little tips
Some craft shops sell adhesive-backed felt, which is easier for younger children to use. Draw your chosen design on the backing paper, then cut it out with scissors. Peel off the backing paper, stick the felt onto the greetings card, and decorate to finish.

You will need:
red wrapping paper • stencil
for motif • white paint • stencil
brush • paper towels • double-
sided sticky tape • cardboard
• hole punch • 40cm/16in
gingham ribbon (1cm/½in wide)

fold paper Cut a rectangular piece of red paper measuring 56cm/22in by 33cm/13in. Fold in 4cm/1½in along one long edge, and 7cm/3in along the other long edge. Fold in the shorter ends by 1.5cm/¾in. Now fold the paper in half so the shorter edges meet, and press flat. Open out again, and on the wrong side of the paper, draw three lines, one 12cm/5in in from one shorter edge, then another at 30cm/12in and a final one at 39cm/15in from the edge. Fold the paper along each line. These folds form the box shape of the bag.

stencil motif Dip the brush in the paint and blot on paper towels to remove any excess paint. If there is too much paint on the brush, the outline will bleed. Hold the stencil over one of the larger panels of the bag (this will be the front) and dab on the paint. Let the paint dry slightly before removing the stencil.

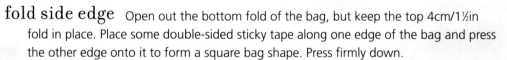

fold side edge Open out the bottom fold of the bag, but keep the top 4cm/1½in fold in place. Place some double-sided sticky tape along one edge of the bag and press the other edge onto it to form a square bag shape. Press firmly down.

fold corners for base Open out the bag, turn it upside down and fold in the long sides to the middle. Fold the corners into triangles, and use double-sided sticky tape to secure them. Cut a piece of card to fit the base and place it inside the bag to strengthen it. Punch two holes on the front and back of the bag just below the top edge and thread two 20cm/8in lengths of ribbon through them. Knot the ends to hold them in place.

stencilled gift bag

What better than to present a hand-made gift in your very own hand-crafted gift bag? These were made from plain wrapping paper and stencilled with a Christmassy candy cane design.

Fun to Bake!

basic recipes

medium cake, to fit an 18-cm/7-in round cake tin/pan

175 g/1½ sticks unsalted butter, softened

175 g/¾ cup plus 2 tablespoons caster/ granulated sugar

3 eggs, lightly beaten

1 teaspoon vanilla extract

175 g/1⅓ cups plain/ all-purpose flour

3 teaspoons baking powder

a pinch of salt

3 tablespoons milk, at room temperature

large cake, to fit a 23-cm/9-in round cake tin/pan

250 g/2 sticks unsalted butter, softened

250 g/1¼ cups caster/ granulated sugar

4 eggs, lightly beaten

1 teaspoon vanilla extract

250 g/2 cups plain/ all-purpose flour

4 teaspoons baking powder

a pinch of salt

3–4 tablespoons milk, at room temperature

This sponge recipe can be baked in almost any shape and tin/pan. It can also be used to make delicious cupcakes – just add frosting.

basic vanilla sponge

1 Preheat the oven to 180°C (350°F) Gas 4. Grease the cake tin/pan you are using.

2 Put the butter and sugar in the bowl of an electric mixer (or use a large bowl and an electric whisk). **Ask an adult to help** you cream them until very pale, light and fluffy.

3 Gradually add the eggs, mixing well between each addition and scraping down the side of the bowl with a rubber spatula from time to time. Add the vanilla extract and mix again.

4 Sift together the flour, baking powder and salt. Add to your mixing bowl and mix again until smooth and well mixed. Add the milk and mix again. Spoon the mixture into the prepared cake tin/pan and spread evenly.

5 **Ask an adult to help** you put the tin/pan on the middle shelf of the preheated oven. Bake until the cake is golden brown, well risen and a skewer inserted into the middle of the cake comes out clean.

Timings will vary according to the recipe that you are using.

Here are some of the frostings and icings that are used throughout the book. Refer to individual recipes for further instructions.

chocolate glaze

175 g/6 oz. dark/ bittersweet chocolate, chopped

1 tablespoon sunflower oil

1 **Ask an adult to help** you put the chocolate and oil in a heatproof bowl over a pan of barely simmering water or in the microwave on a low setting. Stir very carefully until the chocolate has melted, then leave to cool for about 10 minutes before using.

glacé icing

250 g/2 cups icing/ confectioners' sugar

2–3 tablespoons water or lemon juice

1 Sift the icing/confectioners' sugar into a bowl and, using a balloon whisk, gradually stir in enough water or lemon juice to make a smooth icing that will coat the back of a spoon. Add a little more water or juice for a runnier icing.

chocolate frosting

175 g/6 oz. dark/ bittersweet chocolate, chopped

125 g/1 stick unsalted butter, diced

125 ml/½ cup milk

1 teaspoon vanilla extract

225 g/1¾ cups icing/ confectioners' sugar, sifted

1 Ask an adult to help you put the chocolate and butter in a heatproof bowl over a pan of barely simmering water or in the microwave on a low setting. Stir very carefully until melted.

2 Put the milk, vanilla extract and sugar in a mixing bowl and whisk until smooth. Pour the melted chocolate mixture into the mixing bowl and stir until smooth and thickened. You may need to leave this somewhere cool for 30 minutes to thicken enough to spread.

buttercream frosting

350 g/3 sticks unsalted butter, softened

700 g/4½ cups icing/ confectioners' sugar, sifted

1 teaspoon vanilla extract (optional)

1 Put the butter in the bowl of an electric mixer (or use a large bowl and an electric whisk). **Ask an adult to help you** cream it until pale and smooth. Gradually add the sugar and beat until pale and smooth.

2 Add the vanilla extract, if using, and beat until combined.

little treats & gifts

You'll need adult supervision for this recipe when it comes to making the toffee to coat the apples. Look out for small, red-skinned apples, which will make the toffee look even more festive. Why not try dipping the bottoms of the toffee apples in sprinkles or finely chopped toasted nuts before putting them on the parchment to set?

8 small apples, eg Cox's, Jazz or Pink Lady

300 g/1½ cups caster/ granulated sugar

2 tablespoons golden syrup/corn syrup

juice of ½ lemon

finely chopped mixed nuts and edible sprinkles, for dipping (optional)

8 wooden skewers or lolly/popsicle sticks

a large sheet of non-stick baking parchment

makes 8

toffee apples

1 Wash and thoroughly dry each apple. Carefully push a wooden skewer or lolly/ popsicle stick into the stalk end of each apple.

2 Put the sugar, golden/corn syrup and 150 ml/²/₃ cup water in a heavy-based saucepan. **Ask an adult to help you** put it over low heat. Leave until the sugar has completely dissolved.

3 Turn up the heat and simmer until the toffee turns an amber colour.

4 Ask an adult to help you remove the pan from the heat. Carefully add the lemon juice – take care as the hot toffee may splutter. Working quickly, dip each apple into the toffee and swirl it around until evenly coated.

5 Leave to cool for 30 seconds, then dip the bottoms of the apples in mixed nuts or sprinkles, if using. Sit the apples on the baking parchment to harden. Serve on the same day.

Scrumptious, deep, chocolatey brownies that are topped with a delicious chocolate buttercream and scattered with festive sweets.

100 g/²⁄₃ cup walnut pieces

175 g/1½ sticks unsalted butter

250 g/8 oz. dark/bittersweet chocolate, chopped

250 g/1¼ cups sugar

3 eggs

1 teaspoon vanilla extract

150 g/1 cup plus 2 tablespoons plain/all-purpose flour

a pinch of salt

Chocolate Frosting (page 77)

red and green sweets

edible Christmas sprinkles

a 23-cm/9-in square baking tin/pan, greased

makes 16

chocolate brownie squares

1 Preheat the oven to 180°C (350°F) Gas 4.

2 Ask an adult to help you line the prepared baking tin/pan with baking parchment.

3 Put the walnuts on a baking sheet and **ask an adult to help you** put them in the preheated oven. Roast them for 5 minutes, then **ask an adult to help you** remove them from the oven and leave them to cool.

4 Ask an adult to help you put the butter and chocolate in a heatproof bowl over a pan of simmering water. Stir very carefully until it has melted, then leave to cool slightly.

5 Put the sugar and eggs in a mixing bowl. **Ask an adult to help you** use an electric whisk to beat until pale and thick.

6 Add the vanilla and chocolate mixture. Mix well.

7 Sift the flour and salt into the mixing bowl and fold in using a large metal spoon or spatula. Add the roasted walnuts and stir to combine. Pour the batter into the prepared baking tin/pan.

8 Ask an adult to help you put the tin/pan on the middle shelf of the oven. Bake for about 30 minutes. **Ask an adult to help you** remove the tin/pan from the oven, then leave it to cool.

9 Spread the Chocolate Frosting evenly over the brownies. Scatter the sweets and sprinkles over the top, cut into squares and serve.

These buns are traditionally served on St Lucy's day in Sweden, 13th December, where they call them 'lussekatt'. They are normally made into a backwards 'S' shape, but you could make them into any shape you like. Why not have fun with the dough and make simple animal shapes?

swedish saffron buns

250 ml/1 cup milk

a good pinch of saffron strands

500–600 g/4–4¾ cups strong white bread flour

1 x 7-g/¼-oz. sachet easy-blend dried yeast

½ teaspoon salt

50 g/¼ cup caster/ granulated sugar

50 g/3 tablespoons unsalted butter, softened

100 ml/⅓ cup sour cream, at room temperature

1 egg, lightly beaten

24 raisins

2 baking sheets, lined with baking parchment

makes 12

1 Ask an adult to help you heat the milk in a small saucepan until hot but not boiling. Drop the saffron strands in and leave them to infuse in the hot milk for 10 minutes.

2 Tip 500 g/4 cups of the flour, the yeast, salt, sugar, butter and sour cream into a large mixing bowl and stir to mix. Pour the warm milk in and use your hands to mix everything together until you get a dough.

3 To knead the dough, first sprinkle a little flour on a clean work surface. Then shape the dough into a ball and push on it and press it onto the work surface, turning it round often. You'll need to keep doing this until it is silky smooth and elastic – this will take between 4–7 minutes and you may need to add more flour if the dough is too sticky.

4 Shape the dough into a neat ball again. Wash and dry the mixing bowl and sit the dough back in it. Cover with clingfilm/plastic wrap and leave in a warm place until the dough has doubled in size. This can take at least 1 hour.

5 Tip the dough onto the floured work surface and knead for 1 minute. Divide into 12 equal pieces. Roll each piece into a 20-cm/8-inch long sausage and twist into a backwards 'S' shape. Place 6 of the buns on one of the baking sheets and the other 6 on the other sheet.

6 Lightly oil a large sheet of clingfilm/plastic wrap, then use it to loosely cover the baking sheets (oiled-side down). Leave the buns to rise again for a further 30 minutes.

7 Preheat the oven to 190°C (375°F) Gas 5.

8 Brush the buns lightly with the beaten egg and push a raisin into each end of the buns. **Ask an adult to help you** put the sheets on the middle shelf of the preheated oven. Bake for about 12–15 minutes, until well risen, shiny and deep golden brown.

'Lebkuchen' are traditional German Christmas cookies with a good hint of ginger and spices. They can be covered with either a simple white icing or a coating of chocolate.

2 tablespoons clear honey

2 tablespoons black treacle/molasses

40 g/2½ tablespoons unsalted butter

75 g/⅓ cup dark brown soft sugar

grated zest of ½ orange

grated zest of ½ lemon

225 g/1¾ cups self-raising flour

½ teaspoon ground cinnamon

2 teaspoons ground ginger

¼ teaspoon grated nutmeg

a pinch of ground cloves

a pinch of salt

50 g/⅓ cup ground almonds

1 egg, lightly beaten

Chocolate Glaze (page 76)

Glacé Icing (page 76)

edible silver balls

shaped cookie cutters

2 baking sheets, lined with baking parchment

makes about 30

lebkuchen

1 Put the honey, treacle/molasses, butter, sugar and orange and lemon zest in a small saucepan. **Ask an adult to help you** put it over low heat and stir until the butter has melted and everything is well mixed. Carefully remove from the heat and leave to cool.

2 Sift the flour, spices and salt together into a mixing bowl, then add the ground almonds. Add the melted butter mixture and the beaten egg and mix until you get a dough.

3 To knead the dough, sprinkle a little flour on a clean work surface. Shape the dough into a ball and push on it and press it onto the work surface, turning it round often. Do this for just a minute or so until smooth, then wrap in clingfilm/plastic wrap and chill in the fridge for at least 4 hours or overnight.

4 When you are ready to bake the Lebkuchen, preheat the oven to 180°C (350°F) Gas 4. On the floured work surface, roll the dough out to a thickness of 5 mm/¼ inch using a rolling pin. Stamp out shapes with your cookie cutters.

5 Place the Lebkuchen on the prepared baking sheets and **ask an adult to help you** put them in the preheated oven. Bake for about 15–20 minutes, or until just begining to brown at the edges.

6 Ask an adult to help you remove the Lebkuchen from the oven and transfer to a wire rack to cool.

7 When the Lebkuchen are cold, spread Chocolate Glaze or Glacé Icing over them with a palette knife or back of a spoon. Decorate with silver balls or pipe more glaze or icing over the Lebkuchen with a piping bag. (To make a quick piping bag, take a freezer bag and snip off a corner. Fill with glaze or icing and use to pipe lines onto the Lebkuchen.)

Sweet peppermint creams cut into Christmassy shapes make brilliant gifts. Once they have dried out, you can try dipping them in melted dark chocolate and scattering with silver sprinkles. Leave to dry on baking parchment before putting in boxes.

peppermint creams

**225 g/1¾ cups icing/
confectioners' sugar**

**4–6 tablespoons
condensed milk**

**½ teaspoon peppermint
extract**

**green food colouring paste
(optional)**

a mini star-shaped cutter

makes 20–30

1 Sift the icing/confectioners' sugar into a large bowl. Gradually add the condensed milk and peppermint extract, mixing with a wooden spoon. The mixture should come together like dough and you may need to use your hands towards the end of the mixing.

2 To knead the dough, sprinkle a little icing/confectioners' sugar on a clean work surface. Shape the dough into a ball and push on it and press it onto the work surface, turning it round often. Do this for just a minute or so until smooth.

3 If you like, you can divide the dough in half and tint one half green using a little of the food colouring. Knead the dough again until it is evenly green.

4 On the work surface, roll the dough out to a thickness of 4 mm/¼ inch using a rolling pin. Stamp out stars with your cookie cutter and arrange them on a sheet of baking parchment.

5 Leave to dry out overnight before packing into pretty boxes.

These little Italian biscuits are pronounced 'reech-ee-a-relly'. They're chewy and sticky and yummy. You could add a little more finely grated lemon zest or lemon extract in place of the vanilla if you prefer. Dust them in icing/confectioners' sugar, put them in a pretty box and give them to your teacher as a present.

ricciarelli

2 egg whites

a pinch of salt

225 g/1 cup caster/ granulated sugar

grated zest of 1 lemon

½ teaspoon vanilla extract

1 teaspoon almond extract

300 g/2 cups ground almonds

4 tablespoons flaked/ slivered almonds

icing/confectioners' sugar, for dusting

2 baking sheets, lined with baking parchment

makes about 20

1 Preheat the oven to 150°C (300°F) Gas 2.

2 Place the egg whites in a large, clean mixing bowl with the salt. **Ask an adult to help you** use an electric whisk to beat the egg whites until they're nice and thick. When you turn the whisk off and lift them up slowly, the egg whites should stand in stiff peaks.

3 Gradually add the caster/granulated sugar, whisking constantly until completely incorporated. Add the lemon zest, vanilla extract and almond extract and mix again.

4 Fold in the ground almonds using a large metal spoon or spatula.

5 Wet your hands under the tap, then pull off a bit of the dough, about the size of a walnut, and roll it into a ball. Put it on one of the baking sheets and flatten slightly. Keep doing this until you have used all the dough.

6 Sprinkle flaked/slivered almonds over each ricciarelli.

7 Ask an adult to help you put the baking sheets in the centre of the preheated oven. Bake for about 25 minutes, or until pale gold.

8 Ask an adult to help you remove the sheets from the oven. Leave the ricciarelli to cool, then dust with icing/confectioners' sugar.

marshmallow snowmen

200 g/7 oz. large white marshmallows

brown writing icing

coloured liquorice strips or fruit leather

chocolate-coated mint sticks (eg Matchmakers) or pretzel sticks

large chocolate drops

100 g/3½ oz. white mini-marshmallows

icing/confectioners' sugar, for dusting

about 10 cocktail sticks/ toothpicks

makes about 10

1 Place the marshmallows on a tray.

2 Push 2 large marshmallows onto each cocktail stick/toothpick. **Ask an adult to** trim off any of the stick/toothpick that is poking out of the top.

3 Using the writing icing, pipe dots and lines of icing onto the face to make the eyes, nose and mouth.

4 Cut the liquorice strips or fruit leather into thin strips and carefully tie around the snowman's neck for a scarf.

5 To make the arms, break the chocolate-coated mint sticks in half and push into the sides of the large marshmallow.

6 Pipe a small blob of icing onto the top of the snowman's head and position a large chocolate drop on top. Pipe another blob of icing in the middle of the chocolate drop and stick a mini-marshmallow on the very top.

7 Finally, using the writing icing again, pipe dots down the front of the snowman to look like buttons.

8 Keep making snowmen like this until you have as many as you need to make a fabulous winter wonderland!

9 To serve, scatter icing/confectioners' sugar over the serving dish, arrange the snowmen on top and dust lightly with more sugar.

This is definitely a recipe for little hands! These cute chaps are such fun to make and look gorgeous on the Christmas table. Why not make one snowman for each person as a place setting?

This classic treat is so fun to make — and lovely to receive as a gift! Prepare it a day in advance so that it has a chance to dry out before you cut it into small pieces to serve or package prettily into a gift box.

coconut ice

350 g/2¼ cups icing/ confectioners' sugar

400-g/14-oz. can condensed milk

350 g/2⅓ cups desiccated coconut

pink food colouring paste

a 20-cm/8-in square baking tin/pan, lightly greased

makes 25–30

1 Put the icing/confectioners' sugar and the condensed milk in a mixing bowl and mix with a wooden spoon until smooth. Add the coconut and keep mixing until the mixture is well combined – it will get quite stiff!

2 Scoop out half the mixture and place in another mixing bowl. Add a tiny amount of pink food colouring and mix well to colour evenly. Add more colour if you need to.

3 Spread the pink mixture in the prepared tin/pan and make sure it is smooth and flat on top. Spread the white mixture evenly on top. Cover with clingfilm/plastic wrap and leave to dry out overnight.

4 Cut into squares, diamonds or triangles and arrange in a pretty box.

250 ml/1 cup buttermilk

2 eggs

1 teaspoon vanilla extract

350 g/2⅔ cups plain/ all-purpose flour

225 g/1 cup caster/ granulated sugar

1 tablespoon baking powder

1 teaspoon ground cinnamon

a pinch of salt

125 g/1 stick unsalted butter, chilled and diced

75 g/½ cup chopped mixed nuts

250 g/2 cups fresh cranberries

grated zest of 1 orange

25 g/2 tablespoons unsalted butter, melted

a muffin tin/pan, lined with 12 paper muffin cases

makes 12

cranberry streusel muffins

1 Preheat the oven to 180°C (350°F) Gas 4.

2 Put the buttermilk, eggs and vanilla extract in a small bowl and whisk lightly.

3 Put the flour, sugar, baking powder, cinnamon and salt in a large mixing bowl. Add the chilled, diced butter and rub into the dry ingredients using your fingertips. When the mixture looks like breadcrumbs, add the chopped nuts and mix to combine. Scoop out 1 teacupful or roughly 125 g/½ cup of the dry mixture and set aside in a separate bowl.

4 Add the egg mixture to the large bowl and mix until only just combined. Add the cranberries and orange zest and fold in briefly.

5 Spoon the mixture into the muffin cases, filling them almost to the top.

6 Pour the melted butter into the reserved dry ingredients and mix with a fork until crumbly. Scatter evenly over the muffins.

7 Ask an adult to help you put the muffin tin on the middle shelf of the preheated oven. Bake for about 20 minutes or until golden and a wooden skewer inserted into the middle of a muffin comes out clean.

8 Ask an adult to help you remove the muffin tin from the oven. Leave to cool for 2 minutes, then tip the muffins out onto a wire rack to cool completely.

Muffins are super-easy to make and these ones are full of festive cranberries. You could use fresh blueberries, dried cranberries or dried cherries if you prefer.

chocolate truffles

50 g/3 tablespoons unsalted butter, at room temperature

75 g/⅓ cup packed light brown sugar

150 ml/⅔ cup double/ heavy cream

175 g/6 oz. dark/ bittersweet chocolate

Toppings

150 g/5 oz. milk or dark/bittersweet chocolate, chopped

chocolate sprinkles

cocoa powder

edible silver balls

chopped hazelnuts

a baking sheet, lined with baking parchment

makes about 20

1 Ask an adult to help you put the butter, sugar and cream in a saucepan over low heat. Leave until it comes to the boil and the sugar has melted.

2 Break the chocolate into small pieces and tip into a heatproof bowl. Carefully pour the melted butter mixture over the chocolate and stir until the chocolate is melted, smooth and shiny. Leave to cool, then cover with clingfilm/ plastic wrap and chill in the fridge until it's firm.

3 Making one truffle at a time, scoop a teaspoonful of the chocolate mixture and roll quickly between your hands into a ball. Place on the prepared baking sheet.

4 For the toppings, ask an adult to help you put the chocolate in a heatproof bowl over a pan of simmering water or in the microwave on a low setting. Stir very carefully until it has melted. Leave to cool slightly.

5 Sprinkle each of your chosen toppings onto a separate plate.

6 Scoop a teaspoonful of the melted chocolate into the palm of your hand and roll one truffle at a time into it to coat completely.

7 Roll in one of the toppings. Repeat with the remaining truffles and leave to set on the baking sheet before serving or packing into a pretty box.

These truffles make a delicious gift that you can make yourself. Choose between covering them simply with a dusting of cocoa or a variety of nuts and sprinkles.

cranberry & pear relish

300 g/2½ cups fresh cranberries

200 g/1 cup golden caster/granulated sugar

1 cinnamon stick

1 teaspoon ground ginger

grated zest and freshly squeezed juice of 1 orange

4 ripe pears

3 small sterilized jars (see page 4)

makes about 3 jars

1 Put the cranberries, 150 ml/⅔ cup water, the sugar, cinnamon stick, ground ginger and orange zest and juice into a large saucepan. **Ask an adult to help you** put it over medium heat. Cook until the cranberries have softened and burst, then simmer for another 5 minutes.

2 Peel the pears, cut into quarters and remove the cores. Chop the pears into small pieces and add to the pan.

3 Cook for a further 15–20 minutes until the pears are soft and the sauce has thickened.

4 **Ask an adult to help you** remove the pan from the heat. Carefully fish out the cinnamon stick. Taste the sauce and add a little more sugar if needed.

5 Spoon the relish into the sterilized jars, leave to cool, then cover with the sterilized lids. Store in the fridge until needed.

This is the perfect Christmas relish, as it goes well with baked ham or roast turkey. Why not tie the jars up with labels and ribbons and give away as gifts? Keep the relish in the fridge for up to 2 weeks.

iced christmas tree cookies

225 g/2 sticks unsalted butter, softened

225 g/1 cup caster/ granulated sugar

1 egg, lightly beaten

½ teaspoon vanilla extract

a pinch of salt

450 g/3½ cups plain/ all-purpose flour

Glacé Icing (page 76)

assorted coloured writing icing tubes

sugar balls and edible sprinkles

assorted Christmas tree cookie cutters

2 solid baking sheets, lined with baking parchment

makes 12–16, depending on size

1 Put the butter and sugar in the bowl of an electric mixer fitted with the paddle attachment (or use a large bowl and an electric whisk). **Ask an adult to help you** cream them until pale and fluffy. Add the beaten egg, vanilla extract and salt and mix again.

2 Gradually add the flour and mix until incorporated and smooth. Tip the dough out onto the work surface, flatten into a disc, cover with clingfilm/plastic wrap and chill for a couple of hours until firm.

3 Sprinkle a little flour on a clean work surface. Using a rolling pin, roll out the dough to a thickness of about 3–4 mm/⅛ inch. Stamp out shapes with the cookie cutters and arrange on the prepared baking sheets. Gather up any scraps of cookie dough, knead very lightly to bring together into a ball and roll out again to stamp out more cookies. Chill in the fridge for a further 15 minutes.

4 Preheat the oven to 180°C (350°F) Gas 4.

5 **Ask an adult to help you** put the baking sheets on the middle shelf of the preheated oven. Bake for about 10–12 minutes until pale golden and firm to the touch.

6 **Ask an adult to help you** remove the sheets from the oven. Leave the cookies to cool on the baking sheets before transferring to a wire rack to cool completely.

7 When the cookies are cold, use a small palette knife to carefully spread the Glacé Icing over each cookie, trying to keep it as neat as possible. Use the writing icing tubes to pipe tinsel across each cookie. Position the sugar balls and edible sprinkles over the top to look like tree ornaments.

8 Leave the icing to set before serving.

Treat these simple Christmas tree cookies like your own blank canvas to draw any decorative design that you like. Look for colourful edible sprinkles and writing icing pens at the supermarket to help you embellish them.

This is a popular Christmas treat that can either be made the traditional way — in a circle — and cut into wedges, or in a rectangle and then cut into fingers. You could always flavour the basic shortbread dough with lemon zest or even some stem ginger, if you like.

shortbread

175 g/1⅓ cups plain/ all-purpose flour

25 g/3 tablespoons rice flour, fine semolina or cornflour/cornstarch

75 g/⅓ cup caster/ granulated sugar, plus extra for sprinkling

a pinch of salt

175 g/1½ sticks unsalted butter, chilled and diced

a baking sheet, lined with baking parchment

makes 8 wedges

1 Sift the flour, rice flour, sugar and salt into a large mixing bowl. Add the chilled butter and rub in with your fingertips until you get a ball of dough.

2 Sprinkle a little flour on a clean work surface. Tip the dough onto the work surface. Press or roll the dough into a circle about 20 cm/ 8 inches across. Alternatively, you can flatten the dough into a rough rectangle.

3 Carefully lift the shortbread dough onto the middle of the prepared baking sheet.

4 Working your way around the edge of the circle, press the dough between your thumb and forefinger to create a crinkled border.

5 Using a knife, mark 8 wedges into the shortbread, but don't cut all the way through.

6 Chill the shortbread dough in the fridge for 30 minutes.

7 Preheat the oven to 150°C (300°F) Gas 2.

8 Prick the shortbread all over with a fork and sprinkle with more sugar. **Ask an adult to help you** put the baking sheet on the middle shelf of the preheated oven. Bake for about 45–50 minutes until light golden.

9 Ask an adult to help you remove the sheet from the oven. Leave the shortbread to cool a little before cutting into wedges, following the marks you made before baking.

These are filled with a sugary cinnamon butter and topped with a crazy drizzle of icing. Add chocolate chips to the filling for an extra helping of sweetness!

cinnamon sticky buns

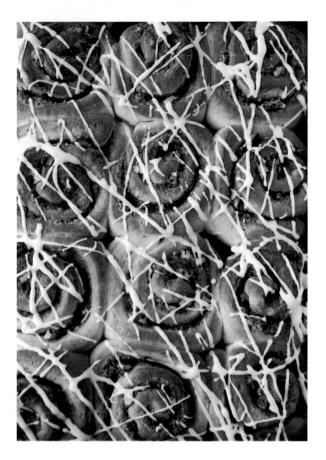

150 ml/⅔ cup milk

500–600 g/4–4¾ cups strong white bread flour

1 x 7-g/¼-oz. sachet easy-blend dried yeast

50 g/¼ cup caster/granulated sugar

a large pinch of salt

2 eggs, lightly beaten

75 g/5 tablespoons unsalted butter, softened

Glacé Icing (page 76)

Filling
100 g/6 tablespoons unsalted butter, softened

100 g/½ cup packed light brown soft sugar

3 teaspoons ground cinnamon

75 g/½ cup pecan pieces

a 23 x 30-cm/9 x 12-in baking tin/pan, greased

makes 12

1 Ask an adult to help you heat the milk in a small saucepan until hot but not boiling.

2 Sift 500 g/4 cups of the flour into a large mixing bowl and stir in the yeast, sugar and salt. Make a well in the middle and pour in the warm milk, eggs and butter. Stir until mixed.

3 To knead the dough, sprinkle a little flour on a clean work surface. Shape the dough into a ball and push on it and press it onto the work surface, turning it round often. You'll need to keep doing this until it is silky smooth and elastic – about 5 minutes – and you may need to add more flour if the dough is too sticky.

4 Shape the dough into a neat ball again. Wash and dry the bowl and sit the dough back in it. Cover tightly with clingfilm/plastic wrap and leave in a warm place until the dough has doubled in size. This will take about 1½ hours.

5 While the dough is rising, make the filling. Put the butter, sugar, cinnamon and pecans in a bowl. Beat with a wooden spoon until mixed.

6 Tip the dough onto the floured work surface and knead lightly for 1 minute. Roll and press it into a rectangle about 30 x 50 cm/12 x 20 inches, with a long side nearest you.

7 Spread the filling over the dough, leaving a border of about 1 cm around the edges.

8 Starting with the side closest to you, roll the dough up evenly and firmly, but not too tight. Cut into 12 slices and place cut-side up in the baking tin/pan. Lightly oil a sheet of clingfilm/plastic wrap, then use it to loosely cover the baking tin/pan (oiled-side down). Leave in a warm place for 30 minutes, or until risen.

9 Preheat the oven to 180°C (350°F) Gas 4.

10 Ask an adult to help you put the tin/pan on the middle shelf of the preheated oven. Bake for 30–35 minutes until golden brown.

11 Ask an adult to help you remove the buns from the oven and leave it to cool completely.

12 Using a spoon, drizzle the Glacé Icing over the buns. Leave to set before tipping them out of the tin/pan and pulling them apart, to serve.

Serve these scrummy squares with a good scoop of the very best vanilla ice cream or pop into your lunchbox for a special treat.

125 g/1 cup plain/
all-purpose flour

50 g/⅓ cup icing/
confectioners' sugar

125 g/1 stick unsalted
butter, chilled and diced

1 egg white

Topping

40 g/3 tablespoons
unsalted butter

150 g/¾ cup packed light
brown soft sugar

3 eggs

1 teaspoon vanilla extract

200 ml/¾ cup maple syrup

100 g/⅔ cup dark/bitter-
sweet chocolate chips

200 g/1⅓ cups pecan
pieces

*a deep, 20-cm/8-in square
baking tin/pan, greased*

makes 16

pecan, toffee & chocolate squares

1 Preheat the oven to 180°C (350°F) Gas 4.

2 Ask an adult to help you put the flour, sugar and butter into a food processor. Using the pulse button, process until the mixture just starts to come together in clumps. Tip the mixture into the prepared baking tin/pan and pat evenly over the bottom of the tin/pan.

3 Ask an adult to help you put the baking tin/pan on the middle shelf of the preheated oven. Bake for 20 minutes, or until pale gold.

4 Ask an adult to help you remove the tin/pan from the oven. Using a pastry brush, very carefully brush the top of the shortbread with the egg white and return to the oven for a further 2 minutes.

5 Ask an adult to help you remove the tin/pan from the oven and leave it to cool while

you prepare the pecan topping. Leave the oven on.

6 To make the topping, **ask an adult to help you** melt the butter in a small saucepan over low heat or in the microwave on a low setting.

7 In a small mixing bowl, whisk together the sugar, eggs, vanilla extract, maple syrup and melted butter with a balloon whisk.

8 Scatter the chocolate chips and pecans over the cooled shortbread base. Pour the filling on top. **Ask an adult to help you** put the baking tin/pan on the middle shelf of the preheated oven. Bake for a further 35 minutes, or until the topping has set.

9 Ask an adult to help you remove the tin/pan from the oven and let cool completely in the tin/pan before cutting into squares to serve.

These pretty snowflakes are simply made from a basic meringue, but add a festive touch with a sprinkling of edible silver glitter or silver balls.

meringue snowflakes

**150 g/¾ cup caster/
granulated sugar**

**75 g/2½ oz. egg whites
(about 2 medium egg
whites)**

edible silver glitter

edible silver balls

*a piping bag, fitted with
a star-shaped nozzle/tip*

*2 solid baking sheets, lined
with baking parchment*

makes about 12

1 Preheat the oven to 200°C (400°F) Gas 6.

2 Tip the sugar into a small roasting tin/pan. **Ask an adult to help you** put the tin/pan in the preheated oven for about 5 minutes until hot to the touch – be careful not to burn your fingers!

3 Turn the oven down to 110°C (225°F) Gas ¼.

4 Place the egg whites in a large, clean mixing bowl or in the bowl of an electric mixer. **Ask an adult to help you** to beat the egg whites (with an electric whisk, if necessary) until they're frothy.

5 Tip the hot sugar onto the egg whites in one go and continue to whisk on high speed for about 5 minutes until the meringue mixture is very stiff, white and cold.

6 Spoon the meringue mixture into the prepared piping bag. Pipe little blobs of meringue onto the prepared baking sheets in the shape of snowflakes. Scatter silver glitter or silver balls over the top.

7 Ask an adult to help you put the sheets in the preheated oven. Bake for about 45 minutes or until crisp and dry. Turn off the oven, leave the door closed and let the snowflakes cool down completely inside the oven.

Topped with a pastry star and filled with cinnamon-spiced apples and cranberries, these little pies are a delicious alternative to mince pies. Use shop-bought sweet pastry to make them in no time at all!

2 cooking apples

2 red eating apples

375 g/12 oz. ready-made sweet pastry/tart dough

50 g/¼ cup caster/granulated sugar, plus extra for sprinkling

½ teaspoon ground cinnamon

juice of ½ lemon

50 g/⅓ cup dried cranberries

1 tablespoon milk

icing/confectioners' sugar, to dust (optional)

a 12-hole tartlet tin/pan

a fluted round cookie cutter, just bigger than the tartlet tin/pan holes

a star-shaped cutter

makes 9–12

apple & cranberry pies

1 Peel both varieties of apple, cut into quarters and remove the cores. Chop the apples into small pieces and tip into a medium saucepan. Add the sugar, cinnamon, lemon juice and cranberries. **Ask an adult to help you** put the pan over low-medium heat, stirring from time to time until the apples are tender.

2 Ask an adult to help you remove the pan from the heat. Taste and add a little more sugar if needed. Set aside until cold.

3 Preheat the oven to 180°C (350°F) Gas 4.

4 Sprinkle a little flour on a clean work surface. Roll out the dough to a thickness of about 2 mm/⅛ inch. Use the fluted cookie cutter to stamp out rounds. Gently press the pastry rounds into the tin/pan holes.

5 Divide the cooled fruit mixture between the pies, filling them almost to the top.

6 Gather up any scraps of dough, knead very lightly to bring together into a ball and roll out again. Use the star-shaped cutter to stamp out stars for the pie tops.

7 Lightly brush the edges of each pie with milk and top with a pastry star. Brush the top of each star with milk and dust with caster/granulated sugar.

8 Ask an adult to help you put the tin/pan on the middle shelf of the preheated oven. Bake for about 25 minutes, or until the pastry is golden brown and the fruit filling is bubbling.

9 Ask an adult to help you remove the tin/pan from the oven. Leave to cool, then dust with icing/confectioners' sugar, if you like.

edible decorations

You will need a selection of numbered cookie cutters, preferably in different sizes, and plain cutters in different shapes to make these. Give them away to friends and family to celebrate Advent.

advent numbered cookies

Vanilla shortbread
225 g/2 sticks unsalted butter, softened

250 g/2 cups plain/all-purpose flour

½ teaspoon salt

75 g/½ cup icing/confectioners' sugar, sifted

1 teaspoon vanilla extract

Chocolate shortbread
225 g/2 sticks unsalted butter, softened

200 g/1⅔ cups plain/all-purpose flour

50 g/⅓ cup cocoa powder

½ teaspoon salt

75 g/½ cup icing/confectioners' sugar, sifted

1 teaspoon vanilla extract

assorted cookie cutters, eg round, square and oval

numbered cookie cutters

1–2 baking sheets, lined with baking parchment

makes about 24

1 To make the vanilla shortbread, beat the butter in a mixing bowl with a wooden spoon until smooth and very soft. Meanwhile, sift together the flour and salt.

2 Add the icing/confectioners' sugar to the creamed butter and continue mixing until light and fluffy. Add the vanilla and mix again. Add the sifted flour and salt and mix until it starts to come together into a dough.

3 To knead the dough, first sprinkle a little flour on a clean work surface. Then shape the dough into a ball and push on it and press it onto the work surface, turning it round often. Do this for a minute, then flatten into a disc, cover with clingfilm/plastic wrap and chill until needed.

4 To make the chocolate shortbread, follow steps 1–3 above, but add the cocoa powder to the flour and salt.

5 Preheat the oven to 180°C (350°F) Gas 4.

6 Sprinkle more flour on the work surface. Using a rolling pin, roll out the vanilla and chocolate dough (separately) to a thickness of 2–3 mm/⅛ inch and stamp out 24 shapes using the assorted cookie cutters. Arrange on the prepared baking sheets. Using the numbered cutters, stamp out numbers 1–24 and stick to each larger cookie with a dab of cold water.

7 Leave the cookies to chill in the fridge for 10 minutes.

8 Ask an adult to help you put one baking sheet on the middle shelf of the preheated oven. Bake for about 12 minutes, or until firm and starting to go crisp at the edges. Repeat with the second sheet of cookies.

9 Ask an adult to help you remove the cookies from the oven and leave to cool on the baking sheets.

This is a very simple, edible Christmas decoration. Why not add some of your favourite candies to the garlands too?

popcorn garlands

sunflower oil, for frying

popcorn kernels

needle and assorted brightly coloured threads

1 Put 1 tablespoon of oil in a large saucepan. **Ask an adult to help you** put it over medium-high heat. Add enough popcorn to cover the base of the pan, cover tightly with a lid and wait for the popping to start.

2 Holding the pan and lid firmly with oven gloves, give the pan a good shake from time to time.

3 When the popping stops, then all the kernels have popped and you can safely take off the lid and remove the pan from the heat. Tip the popcorn into a large bowl and leave to cool.

4 Thread the needle with a long piece of the coloured thread and tie a big, double knot at the end. One by one, push a piece of popcorn onto the thread until you have a long garland. Repeat using different-coloured threads.

5 Arrange the popcorn garlands on the Christmas tree or anywhere that you might need some edible decorations!

While you've got some popcorn on the go, why not make these perfect party nibbles?! They take just moments to make.

popcorn marshmallow clusters

1 tablespoon unsalted butter

125 g/2 cups mini-marshmallows

75–100 g/3½–4 cups popped popcorn

75 g/½ cup pecan pieces

75 g/½ cup dried cranberries

edible silver balls

a baking sheet, lined with baking parchment

makes loads!

1 Put the butter in a large saucepan. **Ask an adult to help you** put it over medium heat. Add the marshmallows and give them a good stir. Once they start to melt, add the popcorn, pecans and cranberries. Stir constantly until the marshmallows melt and the mixture starts to clump together.

2 Carefully tip the mixture out of the pan and onto the prepared baking sheet. Scatter over some edible silver balls.

3 Once the mixture is cool enough to handle, break off clusters and serve in baskets or piled up on plates.

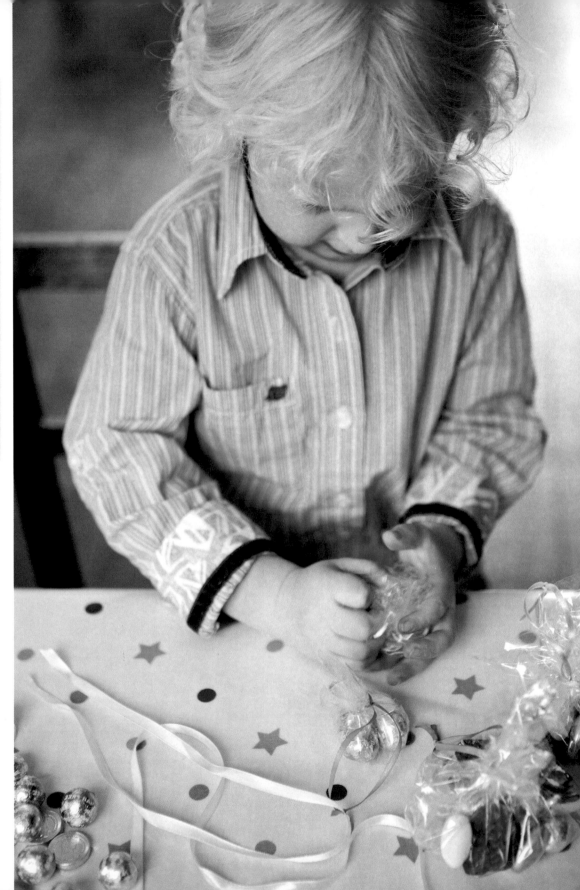

*There's no cooking
required for this
edible, decorative
idea, but it's an easy
and fun way for small
hands to get involved
in the festive fun.*

candy trees

assorted festive candies

roll of clear cellophane or cellophane bags

brightly coloured ribbons

silver spray-painted branches and twigs

1 Tip all the sweets into a large bowl and mix them up!

2 Ask an adult to help you cut large squares from the cellophane. You don't need to do this if you have cellophane bags already. Arrange a handful of sweets in the middle of each square. Gather up the cellophane to make a pouch and tie with pretty festive ribbons, leaving enough ribbon to make a loop.

3 Arrange the silver branches and twigs in a sturdy vase. Hang the parcels on the tree.

Frosted fruit looks wonderfully festive, piled high on a glass serving dish and given pride of place on the dinner table – and it tastes delicious, too. Use a selection of green and red grapes, blueberries and cranberries. In the summer months you could try frosting strands of jewel-like redcurrants.

frosted fruit

**1 egg white or
2 teaspoons dried
egg white mixed with
2 tablespoons warm
water**

**1 bunch of green
grapes**

1 bunch of red grapes

**a handful of
cranberries**

**a handful of
blueberries**

**caster/superfine
sugar, for sprinkling**

*a baking sheet, lined
with baking
parchment*

makes a big plateful

1 Put the egg white or egg white powder and warm water in a large bowl and whisk with a balloon whisk until foamy. Using a pastry brush, brush the egg white over the fruit – try to cover them evenly and completely.

2 Hold the bunches of grapes, one at a time, above the prepared baking sheet and sprinkle sugar over the grapes so that you cover the egg white completely.

3 Lightly brush the cranberries and blueberries with egg white and coat these in sugar too.

4 Leave the fruit to dry on the parchment for at least a couple of hours until the sugar has hardened and become crisp.

5 Arrange the fruit on a platter.

No two snowflakes are the same and these snowflake cookies are no exception. Look out for sets of fancy snowflake cookie cutters in all shapes and sizes and little pots of sparkly edible sprinkles to decorate your cookies with.

snowflake cookies

225 g/2 sticks unsalted butter, softened

225 g/1 cup caster/granulated sugar

1 egg, lightly beaten

½ teaspoon vanilla extract

a pinch of salt

450 g/3½ cups plain/all-purpose flour

Glacé Icing (page 76)

edible white glitter and silver balls

assorted snowflake-shaped cookie cutters

2 baking sheets, lined with baking parchment

makes about 12

1 Put the butter and sugar in the bowl of an electric mixer fitted with the paddle attachment (or use a large bowl and an electric whisk). **Ask an adult to help you** cream them until pale and fluffy. Add the beaten egg, vanilla extract and salt and mix again.

2 Gradually add the flour and mix until incorporated and smooth. Tip the dough out onto the work surface, flatten into a disc, cover with clingfilm/plastic wrap and chill for a couple of hours until firm.

3 Sprinkle a little flour on a clean work surface. Roll out the dough to a thickness of about 5 mm/⅛ inch. Stamp out shapes with the cutters and arrange on the prepared baking sheets. Gather up any scraps of cookie dough,

knead very lightly to bring together into a ball and roll out again to stamp out more cookies. Chill in the fridge for a further 15 minutes.

4 Preheat the oven to 180°C (350°F) Gas 4.

5 Ask an adult to help you put the baking sheets on the middle shelf of the preheated oven. Bake for about 10–12 minutes until pale golden and firm to the touch.

6 Ask an adult to help you remove the sheets from the oven. Leave the cookies to cool on the baking sheets before transferring to a wire rack to cool completely.

7 Make a piping bag as described on page 84. Pipe Glacé Icing onto the cookies and dust with glitter. Decorate with silver balls.

christmas baking

mini baked alaskas

4 x 1-cm/½-in thick slices of shop-bought chocolate loaf cake

2 tablespoons jam or chocolate spread

4 scoops of good-quality vanilla ice cream

2 egg whites

a pinch of salt

125 g/⅔ cup caster/ superfine sugar

a 6-cm/2¼-in round cookie cutter

a baking sheet, lined with baking parchment

makes 4

1 Preheat the oven to 240°C (475°F) Gas 9.

2 Using the cookie cutter, stamp out a round from each slice of chocolate cake and place on the prepared baking sheet. Spread ½ tablespoon jam over each round, top with a scoop of ice cream and freeze.

3 Place the egg whites in a large, clean mixing bowl with the salt. **Ask an adult to help you** use an electric whisk to beat the egg whites until they're nice and thick. When you turn the whisk off and lift them up slowly, the egg whites should stand in stiff peaks.

4 Gradually add the sugar, beating well after each addition, then whisk for a further minute until the meringue is very stiff and glossy.

5 Using a palette knife, cover each ball of ice cream and cake with meringue. **Ask an adult to help you** put the sheet on the middle shelf of the preheated oven. Bake for 2–3 minutes, or until the meringue begins to turn golden at the edges. Serve immediately.

Who doesn't like ice cream and meringue? Put the two together and you've got the perfect pudding. You could use whichever flavour of ice cream you like. Start these puds in advance, keep in the freezer for a couple of hours and simply bake in the oven when you're ready.

This is a thin chocolate sponge which is rolled up and decorated to look like a wooden log. This is traditionally what French people eat for dessert on Christmas Eve. Try it and see if you like it!

bûche de noël

125 g/1 cup self-raising flour

3 tablespoons cocoa powder

4 eggs

150 g/¾ cup caster/ granulated sugar

Chocolate Frosting (page 77)

icing/confectioners' sugar, for dusting

Chocolate bark
150 g/5 oz. chocolate (milk or dark/bittersweet)

a 35 x 25-cm/14 x 10-in Swiss roll tin/jelly roll pan, greased and lined with greased baking parchment

a large sheet of baking parchment, sprinkled with caster/superfine sugar

2 robins, to decorate (optional)

serves 8

1 Preheat the oven to 190°C (375°F) Gas 5.

2 Dust the prepared Swiss roll tin/jelly roll pan with a little flour. Tip out the excess flour.

3 Sift the self-raising flour and cocoa together onto a piece of baking parchment.

4 Break the eggs in the bowl of an electric mixer (or use a large bowl and an electric whisk). Add the sugar and **ask an adult to help you** mix on medium-high speed for about 5 minutes until the mixture is very light, pale and foamy, and has doubled in size.

5 Gently tip the flour and cocoa mixture into the bowl and fold in using a large metal spoon. Carefully tip the mixture into the tin/pan and spread it right to the edges, being careful not to knock out too much air.

6 Ask an adult to help you put the tin/pan on the middle shelf of the preheated oven. Bake for 9–10 minutes until the cake bounces back when lightly pressed with your finger. Be careful not to burn your finger!

7 Ask an adult to help you remove the tin/pan from the oven. Using oven gloves, tip the warm sponge out of the tin/pan and upside down onto the prepared sheet of baking parchment. With one of the long sides nearest you, carefully peel off the parchment. Roll up the sponge with the sugar-dusted paper rolled inside the sponge. Set aside to cool.

8 Make up the Chocolate Frosting as described on page 77. You may need to leave it somewhere cool for 30 minutes to thicken enough to spread.

9 Unroll the sponge and spread the surface with one-third of the frosting. Carefully roll the log back up completely, without the paper this time. Slice one-third off the end at an angle. Arrange the larger piece on a serving plate with the join underneath. Position the smaller third at an angle on one side. Spread the remaining frosting over the cake to cover it.

10 To make the bark, **ask an adult to help you** put the chocolate in a heatproof bowl over a pan of simmering water or in the microwave on a low setting. Stir very carefully until melted.

11 Spread the melted chocolate in a thin layer on a sheet of baking parchment. Leave to set, then break into pieces. Stick the bark onto the log and dust with icing sugar. Decorate with robins, if you like.

This is a delicious French gingerbread cake. Make it a couple of days before you want to eat it so that the flavours of all the spices mixed with the honey will taste much better. Serve it in slices on its own or with a lick of butter.

pain d'épices

225 g/1¾ cups plain/all-purpose flour

2 teaspoons baking powder

1 teaspoon ground cinnamon

3 teaspoons ground ginger

¼ teaspoon ground allspice

¼ teaspoon ground cloves

¼ teaspoon salt

150 g/10 tablespoons unsalted butter, softened

75 g/⅓ cup packed light brown soft sugar

125 ml/½ cup clear honey

2 eggs, lightly beaten

3–4 tablespoons milk

a 2-lb. loaf tin/pan, greased

makes 10 slices

1 Preheat the oven to 180°C (350°F) Gas 4. Base-line the prepared loaf tin/pan with greased baking parchment.

2 Sift the flour, baking powder, cinnamon, ginger, allspice, cloves and salt together into a mixing bowl and set aside.

3 Put the butter and sugar in the bowl of an electric mixer (or use a large bowl and an electric whisk). **Ask an adult to help you** cream them until pale and light.

4 Add the honey and mix again. Gradually add the beaten eggs, mixing well between each addition and scraping down the bowl with a rubber spatula from time to time.

5 Add the sifted dry ingredients and the milk to the bowl and mix again until smooth. Spoon into the prepared tin/pan and spread evenly with a knife.

6 Ask an adult to help you put the tin/pan on the middle shelf of the preheated oven. Bake for about 1 hour, or until well risen and a skewer inserted into the middle of the cake comes out clean. You may need to cover the cake loosely with a sheet of foil if it is browning too quickly.

7 Ask an adult to help you remove the cake from the oven. Leave it to cool in the tin/pan for 5 minutes before tipping out onto a wire rack to cool completely.

Nothing says Christmas like a gingerbread house and this one is straight out of a fairy tale. You could decorate the cake with any number and type of candies, so let your imagination run wild. Be aware that you will need to make up the recipe twice.

gingerbread house

Make up this recipe twice

375 g/3 cups plain/ all-purpose flour

½ teaspoon baking powder

1 teaspoon bicarbonate of soda/baking soda

3 teaspoons ground ginger

½ teaspoon ground cinnamon

¼ teaspoon each of ground cloves and allspice

a pinch of salt

125 g/1 stick unsalted butter, softened

75 g/⅓ cup dark brown soft sugar

1 egg, lightly beaten

100 ml/⅓ cup golden syrup/corn syrup

350–500 g/2–3 cups royal icing sugar

assorted candies

3 solid baking sheets, lined with baking parchment

a piping bag, fitted with a plain nozzle

serves 12

1 Sift the flour, baking powder, bicarbonate of soda/baking soda, ginger, cinnamon, cloves, allspice and salt together into a mixing bowl and set aside.

2 Put the butter and brown sugar in the bowl of an electric mixer (or use a large bowl and an electric whisk). **Ask an adult to help you** cream them until fluffy.

3 Add the beaten egg and golden/corn syrup and mix until smooth. Add the sifted dry ingredients and mix again until smooth.

4 Sprinkle a little flour on a clean work surface. Shape the dough into a ball and push on it and press it onto the work surface, turning it round often. Do this for a minute, then flatten into a disc, cover with clingfilm/plastic wrap and chill in the refrigerator for a couple of hours until firm.

5 Repeat steps 1–4 to make a second quantity of gingerbread dough.

6 When you are ready to bake the house, preheat the oven to 180°C (350°F) Gas 4.

7 You will need to make paper templates for the walls and roof of your house. Take a large sheet of paper and draw a rectangle measuring 20 x 11 cm/8 x 4½ inches for the roof. Make another paper rectangle measuring 19 x 10 cm/ 7½ x 4 inches for the front and back walls. You will also need a template for the sides – this will be a 10-cm/4-inch square with a 4-cm/1½-inch high triangle on top.

8 Sprinkle more flour on the work surface. Using a rolling pin, roll out the dough to a thickness of about 3–4 mm/⅛ inch. Use your paper templates to cut out 2 roof shapes, 2 big walls and 2 sides. You may find it easier to write on the baking parchment which shapes are which as you cut them out. Arrange them on the prepared baking sheets. Carefully cut out windows from the walls and sides.

9 Ask an adult to help you put the sheets on the middle shelf of the preheated oven. You will need to bake the gingerbread in batches. Bake for about 10–15 minutes until firm and just starting to brown at the edges.

10 Ask an adult to help you remove the gingerbread from the oven and leave to cool completely.

11 Use the royal icing sugar to make icing according to the manufacturer's instructions. It will need to be thick enough to hold its shape when piped, so add the water gradually until you have the correct consistency. Fill the piping bag with the icing. You will need 2 pairs of hands for the next step!

12 Take one gingerbread side and pipe a line of icing along the bottom and up one side (just up to but not including the gables). Hold it up on a serving tray or platter. Take a big wall and pipe some icing along the bottom and 2 sides. Hold this at a right angle to the first, iced side. Pick up the second big wall and pipe some icing along the bottom and 2 sides. Hold this in place opposite the other wall and so that it meets the side

at a right angle. Repeat with the remaining side. You may find it easier to position cans or jars inside the house to hold the walls in place until the icing has set firm.

13 Once the walls are completely set and secure, you can attach the roof. Pipe a line of icing down the gables and position one roof panel on either side of the gables. Pipe a line of icing across the top of the roof. Hold the roof in place until the icing feels firm.

14 To decorate the house, pipe royal-icing patterns onto the roof panels and decorate with your choice of candies. Pipe borders around the windows and doors, as well as along the bottom of the house, and decorate with candies as you like.

A classic American holiday recipe that can be whipped up in no time using shop-bought sweet pastry and a can of pumpkin purée.

pumpkin pie

375 g/12 oz. ready-made sweet pastry/pie crust dough

1–2 tablespoons milk

425-g/14-oz. can puréed pumpkin pie filling

2 eggs

1 egg yolk

150 g/⅓ cup packed light brown soft sugar

1 teaspoon ground cinnamon

½ teaspoon ground ginger

a pinch of grated nutmeg

a pinch of ground cloves

a pinch of salt

125 ml/½ cup double/heavy cream

2–3 teaspoons caster/granulated sugar

icing/confectioners' sugar, for dusting

a 23-cm/9-in round pie dish

a small star-shaped cutter

serves 6

1 Preheat the oven to 180°C (350°F) Gas 4 and place a baking sheet on the middle shelf to preheat.

2 Sprinkle a little flour on a clean work surface. Roll out the dough to a thickness of about 2–3 mm/⅛ inch. Carefully lift up the pastry (it may help to lift it while on the rolling pin) and lay it in the pie dish. Carefully trim any excess pastry from around the edge with a small knife.

3 Gather up any scraps of dough, knead very lightly to bring together into a ball and roll out again. Use the star-shaped cutter to stamp out lots of stars. Brush the edges of the pie with a little milk and stick the pastry stars, slightly overlapping, all around the edge.

4 Chill the pastry case in the fridge while you prepare the filling.

5 Put the puréed pumpkin, whole eggs and yolk, brown sugar, cinnamon, ginger, nutmeg, cloves, salt and double/heavy cream in a large bowl and whisk until well mixed and smooth.

6 Carefully pour the mixture into the pie dish, brush the stars with a little more milk and scatter the caster/granulated sugar over them.

7 Ask an adult to help you put the pie on the hot baking sheet in the preheated oven. Bake for about 35 minutes, or until the filling has set and the pastry is golden brown.

8 Ask an adult to help you remove the pie from the oven. Leave to cool to room temperature before dusting with icing/confectioners' sugar.

This is a simple fruit cake that can be decorated any number of ways, but with its crown of sparkling, jewelled dried fruits, it makes a beautiful teatime treat.

easy fruit cake

75 g/½ cup glacé cherries, chopped, plus extra, whole, to decorate

50 g/¼ cup candied mixed peel

450 g/1 lb. mixed dried fruit (eg currants, raisins, chopped dried apricots)

225 g/1¾ cups plain/all-purpose flour

1 teaspoon baking powder

1 teaspoon mixed/apple pie spice

a pinch of salt

175 g/1½ sticks unsalted butter, softened

175 g/¾ cup caster/granulated sugar

3 eggs, lightly beaten

25 g/¼ cup ground almonds

2–3 tablespoons milk

apricot jam, chopped dried apricots, blanched almonds, pecan halves, to decorate

a deep, 20-cm/8-in round cake tin/pan

serves 8–10

1 Preheat the oven to 170°C (325°F) Gas 3. **Ask an adult to help you** line the base and side of the cake tin/pan with a double thickness of baking parchment.

2 Mix the chopped glacé cherries, mixed peel and dried fruit together in a bowl.

3 Sift the flour, baking powder, mixed/apple pie spice and salt together in another bowl.

4 Put the butter and sugar in the bowl of an electric mixer (or use a large bowl and an electric whisk). **Ask an adult to help you** cream them until pale and light.

5 Gradually add the beaten eggs, mixing well between each addition and scraping down the sides of the bowl with a rubber spatula from time to time.

6 Add the dried fruit and stir to mix.

7 Add the sifted dry ingredients and the ground almonds to the mixture and fold in using a large metal spoon or rubber spatula.

8 Add the milk and mix until smooth.

9 Spoon the mixture into the prepared cake tin/pan and spread evenly.

10 Ask an adult to help you put the tin/pan on the middle shelf of the preheated oven. Bake for 30 minutes, then turn the heat down to 150°C (300°F) Gas 2. Continue to bake for a further 1½ hours, or until a skewer inserted into the middle of the cake comes out clean.

11 Ask an adult to help you remove the cake from the oven and leave to cool in the tin/pan.

12 Once the cake is completely cold, tip it out of the tin/pan and carefully peel off the paper.

13 Ask an adult to help you put about 5 tablespoons apricot jam in a small saucepan over low heat. Leave until runny, then pass the jam through a sieve/strainer to remove any lumps.

14 Brush the top of the cake with a thin layer of the jam. Arrange the glacé cherries, apricots and nuts in a pretty pattern on top. Brush with a little more jam to glaze, then leave to set.

This is the perfect cake for a Christmas party, as it will feed a good crowd of hungry mouths.

frosty the snowman

Medium Cake (page 76)

Large Cake (page 76)

Buttercream Frosting (page 77)

red food colouring paste

300 g/4 cups desiccated coconut

1 large cupcake (store-bought or home-made)

1 plain liquorice allsort/short licorice twizzler

chocolate chips

4 red sugar-coated sweets

40 g/1½ oz. white ready-to-use fondant or royal icing

orange food colouring paste

2 short lengths of flaked chocolate

an 18-cm/7-in round cake tin/pan, greased and base-lined with greased baking parchment

a 23-cm/9-in round cake tin/pan, greased and base-lined with greased baking parchment

a length of ribbon

serves at least 14

1 Preheat the oven to 180°C (350°F) Gas 4.

2 Make up the Medium Cake and Large Cake as described on page 76. Spoon the medium cake batter into the prepared 18-cm/7-inch cake tin and the large cake batter into the 23-cm/9-inch cake tin/pan. Spread evenly.

3 Ask an adult to help you put the tins/pans on the middle shelf of the preheated oven. Bake the medium cake for about 30 minutes and the large cake for 35–40 minutes, or until a skewer inserted into the middle of the cakes comes out clean.

4 Ask an adult to help you remove the tins/pans from the oven and leave to cool for 10 minutes before tipping the cakes out to cool on a wire rack.

5 While the cakes are cooling, take the Buttercream Frosting and put 5 tablespoons into a small bowl. Tint this small amount red using the red food colouring paste.

6 Lay the cold cakes side by side. If necessary, cut a thin layer off the tops of the cakes so that they are the same height. Cut away about one-fifth off the larger cake in an inward curve and set aside. Lay the ribbon down horizontally before fitting the smaller cake on the ribbon into the curved space.

7 Cover the top and side of both of the cakes in the untinted buttercream, spreading it evenly with a palette knife. Cover the whole cake evenly in desiccated coconut.

8 Use the reserved leaf-shaped piece of cake and the cupcake to make the snowman's hat. Cover these in the red buttercream and position on top of the snowman's head.

9 Cut the liquorice allsort/twizzler in half for the eyes and arrange the chocolate chips for the mouth. Position the sugar-coated sweets down the centre as buttons.

10 Tint the fondant icing orange using the food colouring paste and shape this into a carrot. Position on the snowman's face.

11 Finally, push a length of flaked chocolate into each side for the snowman's arms.

party food

You could easily serve these as a fancy starter on Christmas day. The pancakes can be made in advance and frozen – simply wrap them in foil and warm in the oven before serving.

scotch pancakes with smoked salmon

125 g/1 cup plain/ all-purpose flour

1 teaspoon baking powder

a large pinch of salt

1 egg

150–200 ml/⅔–¾ cup milk

1–2 tablespoons sunflower oil

To serve
200 g/7 oz. smoked salmon

10 teaspoons crème fraîche or sour cream

1 tablespoon finely snipped chives

makes about 20

1 Sift the flour, baking powder and salt into a large mixing bowl. Break the egg into the bowl and gradually pour in the milk, mixing all the time with a balloon whisk. You may not need to add all the milk – the batter should be smooth and thick.

2 Ask an adult to help you preheat a griddle pan or heavy frying pan over medium heat. Pour a little of the oil in the pan and swirl it to coat the base of the pan evenly. Leave it to heat up.

3 Drop a tablespoon of batter into the hot pan for each pancake – you will probably only be able to cook 4 pancakes at a time. Cook for about 1 minute, or until bubbles start to appear on the surface and the underside is golden. Using a fish slice or palette knife, flip the pancakes over and cook the other side until the pancakes are golden.

4 Remove the pancakes from the pan and keep them warm on a plate covered with foil.

5 Repeat with the remaining batter.

6 To serve, snip the smoked salmon into pieces. Dollop ½ teaspoon crème fraîche onto each pancake and top with the salmon. Finish with a sprinkle of snipped chives.

No party is complete without a heaped dish of hot bite-sized sausage rolls. All you need to add is a bowl of ketchup to serve with them.

sausage rolls

375 g/12 oz. ready-rolled puff pastry dough

1 tablespoon Dijon mustard

24 cocktail sausages

1 egg, lightly beaten

a baking sheet, lined with baking parchment

makes 24

1 Preheat the oven to 190°C (375°F) Gas 5.

2 Sprinkle a little flour on a clean work surface. Unroll the pastry, and if it's thicker than 2 mm/⅛ inch, use a rolling pin to make it the right thickness. Spread the mustard over the pastry.

3 With the long side of the pastry nearest you, cut the pastry vertically into 6 equal strips. Cut each strip into 4. Place a sausage on each piece of pastry and roll the pastry around it. Arrange on the prepared baking sheet.

4 Score 2 or 3 small cuts in the top of each sausage roll with a sharp knife and brush with the beaten egg.

5 Ask an adult to help you put the sheet on the middle shelf of the preheated oven. Bake for 30 minutes, or until golden.

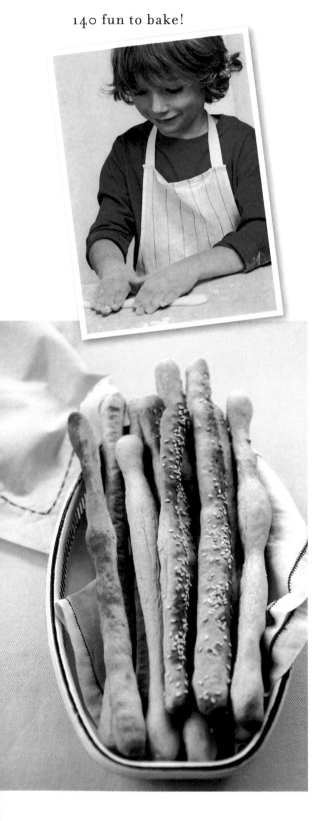

These Italian-style grissini sticks have Parmesan added to the dough to make them a little more interesting. Grissini are delicious eaten on their own or served with dips or soup.

cheesy grissini

375 g/3 cups strong white bread flour

1 x 7-g/¼-oz sachet easy-blend dried yeast

1 teaspoon fine sea salt

200 ml/¾ cup warm water

1 tablespoon olive oil

3 tablespoons finely grated Parmesan

1–2 tablespoons sesame seeds (optional)

2 or more baking sheets, lined with baking parchment

makes about 24

1 Sift the flour into a large mixing bowl and stir in the yeast and salt. Make a hole like a well in the middle and pour in three-quarters of the water and all the oil. Stir with a wooden spoon – the dough should be soft but not too sticky.

2 Add the grated Parmesan to the dough. It will get mixed in when you knead the dough.

3 To knead the dough, sprinkle a little flour on a clean work surface. Shape the dough into a ball and push on it and press it onto the work surface, turning it round often. You'll need to keep doing this until it is silky smooth and elastic – about 7 minutes.

4 Shape the dough into a neat ball again. Wash and dry the mixing bowl and sit the dough back in it. Cover tightly with clingfilm/plastic wrap and leave in a warm place until the dough has doubled in size. This can take at least 1 hour.

5 Preheat the oven to 200°C (400°F) Gas 6.

6 Tip the dough onto the floured work surface and knead for 1 minute. Divide it into walnut-sized pieces and roll each piece into a long stick using your hands. Arrange on the prepared baking sheets and leave to rise again for a further 10 minutes.

7 Brush some of the grissini with water and sprinkle the sesame seeds over them, if using.

8 Ask an adult to help you put one of the sheets on the middle shelf of the preheated oven. Bake for 7–8 minutes, or until crisp and golden brown.

9 Repeat with the remaining grissini.

French toast is such a nice thing to have as a treat for breakfast. Why not surprise your family and make a batch for everyone early on Christmas morning? You will need just a little help from an adult.

french toast

4 eggs

4 tablespoons milk

a good pinch of ground cinnamon

1 teaspoon vanilla extract

1 tablespoon maple syrup, plus extra for drizzling

12 slices of brioche, white bread or panettone

4 tablespoons unsalted butter

icing/confectioners' sugar, for dusting

a star-shaped cookie cutter

serves 4

1 Put the eggs, milk, cinnamon, vanilla and maple syrup in a mixing bowl and whisk with a balloon whisk.

2 Lay the bread slices out on a chopping board and, using the star-shaped cutter, stamp out a star from the middle of each slice.

3 Ask an adult to help you melt half the butter in a large non-stick frying pan over medium-high heat.

4 Dip half the bread stars into the egg mixture and allow to soak thoroughly on both sides.

5 Add the eggy stars to the hot pan – you will need to fry them in batches because you should have just one layer of stars in the pan at a time. Cook for about 1 minute or until they turn golden.

6 Turn the stars over and cook the other sides for another minute.

7 Repeat with the remaining butter and stars. You will have 3 per person. Dust with icing/confectioners' sugar and drizzle with maple syrup to serve.

**225 g/1¾ cups plain/
all-purpose flour**

**2 teaspoons baking
powder**

a pinch of salt

**½ teaspoon mustard
powder (optional)**

**50 g/3 tablespoons
unsalted butter, chilled
and diced**

**50 g/½ cup grated
Cheddar, plus extra for
sprinkling**

50 g/½ cup diced ham

1 egg, lightly beaten

75–100 ml/⅓–½ cup milk

*a 6-cm/2-in round cookie
cutter*

*a baking sheets, lined with
baking parchment*

makes 8–10

cheese & ham scones

1 Preheat the oven to 200°C (400°F) Gas 6.

2 Sift the flour, baking powder, salt and mustard powder, if using, into a large mixing bowl. Add the chilled, diced butter and rub in using your fingertips.

3 Add three-quarters of the cheese and all the ham and mix well. Make a hole like a well in the middle. Pour in the beaten egg and enough milk to make a soft dough.

4 Sprinkle a little flour on a clean work surface. Use a rolling pin to roll out the dough until it is about 2 cm/¾ thick. Stamp out rounds with the cookie cutter and arrange the scones on the prepared baking sheet.

5 Brush the scones with a little milk and scatter a little more cheese over the tops. **Ask an adult to help you** put the sheet on the middle shelf of the preheated oven. Bake for about 10–12 minutes until golden brown.

6 Ask an adult to help you remove the sheet from the oven and tip the scones onto a wire rack to cool.

Scones are so delicious
and so easy to make.
Serve these little
cheesy nuggets still
warm from the oven
or with a bowl of
steaming soup.

bagel chips

4 plain bagels

3–4 tablespoons olive oil

sea salt flakes

2 teaspoons dried oregano

1 teaspoon smoked paprika

2 tablespoons grated Parmesan

makes about 32

1 Preheat the oven to 180°C (350°F) Gas 4.

2 Cut each bagel in half to make semi-circles. Put one half cut-side down and very carefully slice the bagel vertically, as thinly as possible. Repeat with the remaining bagels and lay the slices on baking sheets in a single layer. Brush each slice with olive oil. Sprinkle a quarter of the slices with salt, a quarter with oregano, a quarter with paprika and a quarter with cheese.

3 Ask an adult to help you bake them in the preheated oven for 15 minutes, or until golden and crisp.

savoury dips

Dips are perfect for parties – serve them with Bagel Chips (opposite).

red pepper & chickpea dip

2 red bell peppers

2 tablespoons olive oil

420-g/14-oz. can of chickpeas

juice of ½ lemon

1 rounded tablespoon Greek yogurt

1 small garlic clove, crushed (optional)

a pinch of cayenne pepper (optional)

sea salt and freshly ground black pepper

makes a bowlful

1 Preheat the grill/broiler.

2 Cut the peppers in half and scoop out the seeds with a spoon. Arrange the peppers on a baking sheet, skin-side up. Drizzle with the olive oil and **ask an adult to help you** put them under the hot grill/broiler. Grill until the skins of the peppers are blackened and charred. Tip the hot peppers into a bowl, cover with clingfilm/plastic wrap and leave to cool for about 10 minutes.

3 When the peppers are cool, peel off the skins and throw them away. Put the peppers in a food processor. Drain the chickpeas and rinse under cold water. Add to the peppers. Add the lemon juice, yogurt, garlic and cayenne, if using, and season with salt and pepper.

4 **Ask an adult to help you** whizz the ingredients until they are almost smooth. Taste and add more lemon, salt or pepper if you like.

avocado dip

2 ripe avocados

1 ripe tomato

juice of 1 lemon

a dash of Worcestershire sauce

sea salt and freshly ground black pepper

makes a bowlful

1 **Ask an adult to help you** cut the avocados in half and remove the stones/pits. Use a spoon to scoop out the flesh from each half and place in a mixing bowl. Mash the avocado with a fork until it is almost smooth.

2 Chop the tomato into small pieces and add to the avocado with the lemon juice and Worcestershire sauce. Mix well, then season with salt and pepper.

cream cheese & herb dip

300 g/1¼ cups cream cheese

3 tablespoons Greek yogurt

juice of ½ lemon

1 tablespoon finely chopped parsley

1 tablespoon finely snipped chives

1 small garlic clove, crushed (optional)

sea salt and freshly ground black pepper

makes a bowlful

1 Put the cream cheese in a mixing bowl and beat with a wooden spoon until slightly softened. Stir in the yogurt, lemon juice, herbs and garlic, if using. Season to taste with salt and pepper.

Palmiers can be savoury or sweet. These ones are filled with pesto and grated Parmesan, but you could also try scattering the rolled-out pastry with caster sugar and cinnamon.

pesto palmiers

375 g/12 oz. ready-rolled puff pastry dough

2 tablespoons red pesto

2 tablespoons green pesto

100 g/1 cup grated Parmesan

50 g/½ cup grated Cheddar

1 egg, beaten

makes about 24

1 Sprinkle a little flour on a clean work surface. Use a rolling pin to roll out the dough to a rectangle just over 50 x 25 cm/20 x 10 inches. Using a large knife, trim the edges of the rectangle and then cut the pastry in half lengthways to give 2 squares measuring roughly 25 x 25 cm/10 x 10 inches.

2 Spread the red pesto over one square and green pesto over the other. Scatter some grated Parmesan and Cheddar evenly over each square of pastry.

3 Take one square and fold the sides in towards the middle until they meet. Brush the top with a little beaten egg. Fold the sides in again to meet in the middle, then brush with more egg and fold in again. The pastry should now be in a long, thin roll. Place on a baking sheet and set aside while you do the same with the other square of pastry.

4 Chill the rolls in the fridge for 30 minutes.

5 Preheat the oven to 180°C (350°F) Gas 4.

6 Cut the pastry rolls into 1-cm/½ inch slices and arrange the slices in a single layer on 2 baking sheets. Slightly flatten each palmier. **Ask an adult to help you** put one sheet on the middle shelf of the oven. Bake for about 20 minutes, or until golden and crisp.

7 Repeat to bake the second sheet of palmiers.

Cheesy and just a little bit spicy,
these straws are nice with a mug
of Mulled Apple Juice (page 152).

These nuts can be made well in advance and stored in an airtight container. Use unsalted and unroasted nuts from the baking section of the supermarket and feel free to vary the selection to include hazelnuts and walnuts, if you prefer.

200 g/1⅓ cups shelled Brazil nuts

100 g/⅔ cups shelled almonds

100 g/⅔ cups shelled pecan nuts

½ teaspoon cayenne pepper

½ teaspoon ground cinnamon

2 tablespoons olive oil

2 teaspoons sugar

½ teaspoon sea salt flakes

freshly ground black pepper

serves 6

spiced nuts

1 Preheat the oven to 190°C (375°F) Gas 5.

2 Mix all the ingredients together well.

3 Spread evenly in a single layer on a baking sheet. **Ask an adult to help you** put the sheet on the middle shelf of the oven. Bake for about 10 minutes, or until golden and crisp.

4 Ask an adult to help you remove the sheet from the oven and leave to cool slightly before serving.

125 g/1 cup plain/ all-purpose flour

a pinch of sea salt

½ teaspoon cayenne pepper

½ teaspoon mustard powder

100 g/6½ tablespoons unsalted butter, chilled and diced

100 g/1 cup grated mixed grated mature/sharp Cheddar and Parmesan

a baking sheet, lined with baking parchment

makes about 24

cheese straws

1 Sift the flour, salt, cayenne and mustard powder into the bowl of a food processor. Add the butter. **Ask an adult to help you** pulse the ingredients until they look like breadcrumbs.

2 Add the grated cheeses and pulse again until the dough starts to come together into a ball.

3 To knead the dough, sprinkle a little flour on a clean work surface. Shape the dough into a ball and push on it and press it onto the work surface. Do this very briefly, just to bring the dough together. Flatten into a disc, cover with clingfilm and chill in the fridge for 30 minutes.

4 Preheat the oven to 190°C (375°F) Gas 5.

5 Tip the dough onto the floured work surface and roll out with a rolling pin until it is about 6–7 mm/⅜ inch thick. Cut into 1-cm/½ inch wide strips and arrange on the prepared baking sheet.

6 Ask an adult to help you put the sheet on the middle shelf of the oven. Bake for about 12 minutes, or until golden.

7 Ask an adult to help you remove the sheet from the oven and leave to cool slightly before serving.

christmas drinks

hot chocolate

**40 g/1½ oz. dark/
semisweet chocolate drops**

350 ml/1⅓ cups whole milk

a few drops vanilla extract

**2 teaspoons sugar or
honey, or to taste**

**1 tablespoon whipped
double/heavy cream or
squirty cream from a can**

mini-marshmallows

serves 1

1 Tip the chocolate drops into a heatproof glass or mug.

2 Put the milk, vanilla extract and sugar in a small saucepan. **Ask an adult to help you** set it over medium heat and heat until just boiling, then whisk with a balloon whisk until foamy.

3 Pour the hot milk over the chocolate drops and stir until the chocolate has melted. Taste and add a little more sugar if needed.

4 Dollop the cream on the top, scatter with mini-marshmallows and serve immediately.

mulled apple juice

**1 litre/4 cups cloudy
apple juice**

1 cinnamon stick

4 whole cloves

2 tablespoons clear honey

1 orange

**2–3 small Cox's or Macoun
apples**

makes about 1 litre/4 cups

1 Pour the apple juice into a saucepan and add the cinnamon stick, whole cloves and honey.

2 Remove the zest from the orange in strips using a vegetable peeler and add to the pan.

3 Cut the apples into quarters and remove the cores. Thinly slice the apples and tip them into the apple juice. **Ask an adult to help you** put the pan over medium heat and bring the juice to a gentle simmer. Cook for 5 minutes.

4 Ladle the mulled apple juice into cups or mugs and serve.

These are perfect drinks to warm you up when it's chilly outside. The hot chocolate is made with real chocolate and a few drops of vanilla extract to make it that little bit more special. The mulled apple juice is your opportunity to join in with the adults when they indulge in their own spiced mulled wine!

templates

(cut out centre)

pompom disc
(pages 10–11)
cut two in cardboard

small heart for centre of 3-D card
(page 56)

heart for 3-D card
(page 56)

star for 3-D card
(pages 54–55)
and hanging felt stars
(pages 40–43)

bell for 3-D card
(page 57)

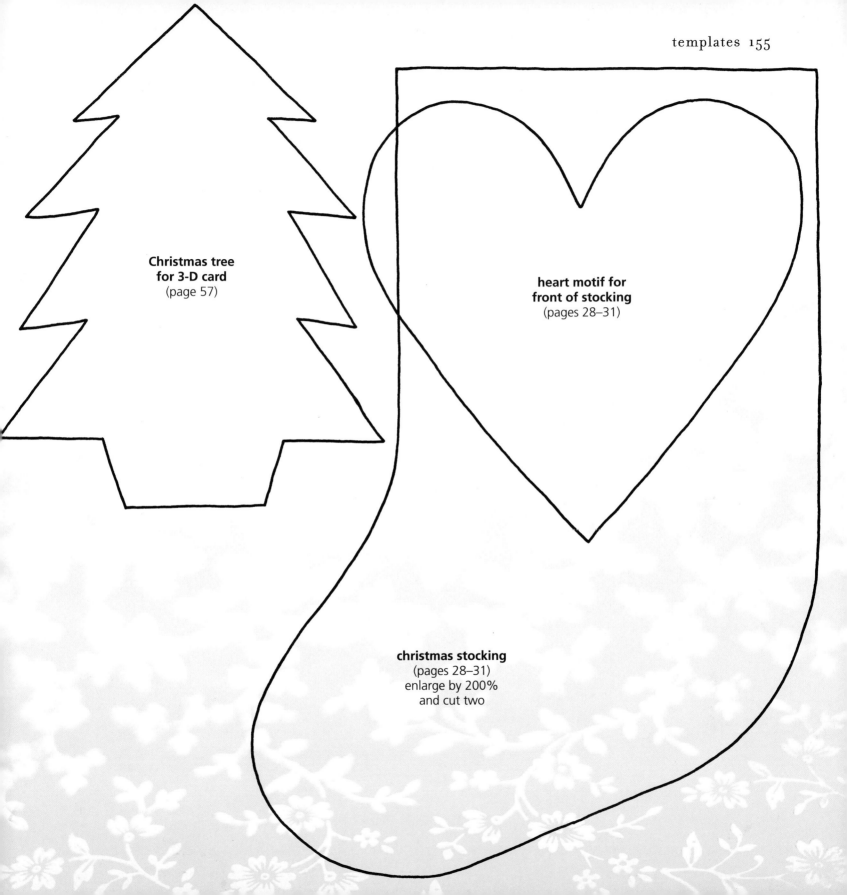

**Christmas tree
for 3-D card**
(page 57)

**heart motif for
front of stocking**
(pages 28–31)

christmas stocking
(pages 28–31)
enlarge by 200%
and cut two

sources

UK

CALICO CRAFTS

www.calicocrafts.co.uk
*Online crafts specialist
with large stock of crafting
materials. Also vintage-style
labels that are ideal for
découpage projects.*

CREATIONS ART AND CRAFTS MATERIALS

01326 555777
www.ecreations.co.uk
*Online craft store with large
stock of Christmas-themed
rubber stamps and stencils,
paints, glue and more.*

EARLY LEARNING CENTRE

Visit www.elc.co.uk for
details of your nearest store.
*Their large craft section
includes funky-coloured
paints, paintbrushes, felt-tip
pens, scissors, glitter pens,
glue, pompoms, coloured
feathers and simple stencils.*

THE ENGLISH STAMP COMPANY

www.englishstamp.com
*Traditional wooden stamps,
including a good selection
of Christmassy stamps in
various sizes. Also ink pads.*

HOBBYCRAFT

Visit www.hobbycraft.co.uk
for details of your nearest
store.
*Chain of craft superstores,
carrying everything the
young crafter needs: ribbons,
pompoms, air-drying clay,
blank cards and envelopes,
Christmas stamps and ink
stamp pads, sequins, buttons
and beads, plus much more.*

HOMECRAFTS DIRECT

0116 269 7733
www.homecraftsdirect.co.uk
*Log on here to order hard-to-
find items such as tinsel pipe
cleaners, plain wooden
frames and cracker snaps,
as well as all the necessary
craft staples, including crêpe
paper, plain and coloured
doilies, glue sticks, glue
guns, fabric paints and air-
drying clay.*

IKEA

Visit www.ikea.com for a
catalogue or details of your
nearest store.
*Good selection of wooden
boxes and files and plain
picture frames in unfinished
wood that are ready for
painting and decorating.
Also seasonal selections of
fun decorations, wrapping
paper and cards.*

JANE ASHER PARTY CAKES AND SUGARCRAFT

24 Cale Street
London SW3 3QU
020 7584 6177
www.jane-asher.co.uk
*Excellent selection of novelty-
shaped cookie cutters in
both metal and plastic, plus
cake decorations, cake frills,
a variety of pretty paper
doilies and coloured cake
cases in many different sizes.*

JOHN LEWIS

Visit www.johnlewis.com for
details of your nearest store.
*John Lewis haberdashery
departments offer embroidery
threads and cottons in many
colours, as well as craft
essentials including felt, pipe
cleaners, ribbons, ricrac
braid and sequins.*

LAKELAND LTD

Visit www.lakelandlimited.com
for your nearest store.
*Stocks crafting products
such as blank cards and
envelopes, ribbons, card kits
and a large selection of
decorative stamps and inks.
Also a specialist in kitchen
utensils such as cookie
cutters, cake tins, icing
cutters, chocolate moulds
and edible glitter and cake
sprinkles.*

PAPERCHASE

Visit www.paperchase.co.uk
for details of your nearest
store.
*Large selection of hand-
made papers, crêpe and
tissue paper and metallic
card. Also 3-D paint, glitter
glue pens, and blank cards
and envelopes in many
colours and sizes.*

VV ROULEAUX

6 Marylebone High Street
London W1M 3PB
020 7224 5179
Visit www.vvrouleaux.com for
details of their other stores.
*A vast selection of ribbons
from taffeta and velvet to
embroidered cotton, plus
pompoms, pretty trims
and fabric flowers.*

THE STENCIL LIBRARY

www.stencil-library.com
*Decorative stencils, from
simple festive shapes to
more complicated designs,
plus stencil paints and
brushes. Paints can be used
on walls, furniture and fabric.*

URCHIN

Call 0870 112 6006
or visit www.urchin.co.uk for
details of your nearest store.
Bumper craft packs.

USA

A.C. MOORE

Visit www.acmoore.com for details of your nearest store.
Craft superstores carrying modelling clay, pipe cleaners, stencils, paper doilies, and natural wooden frames.

THE BUTTON EMPORIUM & RIBBONRY

1016 SW Taylor Street
Portland, OR 97205
503-228-6372
www.buttonemporium.com
Vintage and assorted decorative buttons and a huge range of ribbon.

CANDYLAND CRAFTS

201 West Main Street
Somerville, NJ 08876
908-685-0410
www.candylandcrafts.com
Baking and muffin cups, cookie cutters, edible cake decorations, fondant icing, piping gel, and sugar paste.

CHRISTMAS CRACKERS USA

www.christmas-crackers-usa.com
Ready-made party crackers as well as components such as cracker snaps, cardboard tubes and paper hats.

DICKBLICK

Visit www.dickblick.com for details of your nearest store.
Cardmaking supplies, crepe, tissue, and decorative paper, stencils, ribbon, and more.

HOBBY LOBBY

Visit www.hobbylobby.com for details of your nearest store.
Crafts retailer stocking a large selection of general crafts materials.

IKEA

Visit www.ikea.com for a catalogue or details of your nearest store.
Good selection of wooden boxes and files and plain picture frames in unfinished wood that are ready for painting and decorating. Also seasonal selections of fun decorations, wrapping paper and cards.

JAM PAPER

www.jampaper.com
Paper, card, and envelopes of all sizes and customized rubber stamps.

JO-ANN FABRICS

Visit www.joann.com for details of your nearest store.
A wide selection of paper, card, fabric, and more.

KARI ME AWAY

www.karimeaway.com
Rickrack trim in a large variety of colours, as well as a good selection of novelty buttons and glass beads.

KATE'S PAPERIE

72 Spring Street
New York, NY 10012
800-809-9880
www.katespaperie.com
Cute rubber stamps for kids.

MICHEALS

Visit www.michaels.com for details of your nearest store.
Large craft supplier stocking an enormous range of craft materials, including beads, air-drying modelling clay, stamps, hole punches, ink pads, embellishments, glue, and paints.

M&J TRIMMING

www.mjtrim.com
Fancy trims, including rhinestones, sequined flowers, ribbons, lace, rosettes and beaded braid.

PAPER CREATIONS

www.papercreations.com
Supplies for papercrafting and scrapbooking as well as rubber stamps.

PEARL ART AND CRAFTS SUPPLIES

Visit www.pearlpaint.com for details of your nearest store.
Brushes, modeling clay, adhesives, papers and card.

TARGET

Visit www.target.com for details of your nearest store.
Paper, scrapbooking accessories, tools, and more.

TINSEL TRADING CO.

1 West 37th Street
New York, NY 10018
212-730-1030
www.tinseltrading.com
Vintage buttons and beads, as well as gorgeous silk and velvet flowers, sequins, metallic tassels and ribbons.

THE ULTIMATE BAKER

866-285-COOK
www.cooksdream.com
Online cake-decorating supply store. Cookie cutters, food colouring, edible ink, and rolled fondant in many colours.

UTRECHT

Visit www.utrechtart.com for details of your nearest store.
Quality artists' materials and supplies, including modelling clay, paints, and craft paper.

index

credits

Project credits

Catherine Woram:
3-D christmas cards
Angel tree topper
Beaded decorations
Candle centrepiece
Christmas crackers
Christmas stocking
Cinnamon sticks
Clay decorations
Découpaged tin
Felt motif cards
Hanging felt stars
Mini tree
Orange pomanders
Orange tree decorations
Paperchains
Paper lanterns
Paper snowflakes
Pompom tree decorations
Potato print wrapping paper
Snow globes
Stamped gift tags
Stencilled gift bag
Twiggy wreath

Annie Rigg:
Advent numbered cookies
Apple & cranberry pies
Avocado dip
Bagel chips
Basic vanilla sponge
Bûche de Noel
Buttercream frosting
Candy trees
Cheese & ham scones
Cheese straws
Cheesy grissini
Chocolate brownie squares
Chocolate frosting
Chocolate glaze
Chocolate truffles
Christmas drinks
Cinnamon sticky buns
Coconut ice
Cranberry & pear relish
Cranberry streusel muffins
Cream cheese & herb dip
Easy fruit cake
French toast
Frosted fruit
Frosty the snowman
Gingerbread house
Glacé icing
Iced Christmas tree cookies
Lebkuchen
Marshmallow snowmen
Meringue snowflakes
Mini baked Alaskas
Pain d'épices
Pecan, toffee & chocolate squares
Peppermint creams
Pesto palmiers
Popcorn garlands
Popcorn marshmallow clusters
Pumpkin pie
Red pepper & chickpea dip
Ricciarelli
Sausage rolls
Scotch pancakes with smoked salmon
Shortbread
Snowflake cookies
Spiced nuts
Swedish saffron buns
Toffee apples

Photography credits

Lisa Linder: pages 1, 2, 7 above right, 7 below right, 74–153

Polly Wreford: pages 3, 4–5, 6 above left, 6 below left, 6 below centre, 8–73

Ryland Peters & Small would like to thank all the children that appear as models in this book: Aimee, Alessandra, Alissia, Amelia, Anna, Archie, Ayesha, Bella, Bluebelle, Cameron, Celia, Chantal, Charlie, Constance & Lydia, David, Donnell-Andre, Ella & Ben, Emma & Julian, Hannah, Hassia, Honor, Imani & India, Jack, Jago, Jessica, Kai, Mackie, Malise, Marly, Max & Timmy, Parisa, Polly & Will, Saffron, Saskia, Thomas & Ollie, Tom, Tommy and William.

credits

Project credits

Catherine Woram:
3-D christmas cards
Angel tree topper
Beaded decorations
Candle centrepiece
Christmas crackers
Christmas stocking
Cinnamon sticks
Clay decorations
Découpaged tin
Felt motif cards
Hanging felt stars
Mini tree
Orange pomanders
Orange tree decorations
Paperchains
Paper lanterns
Paper snowflakes
Pompom tree decorations
Potato print wrapping paper
Snow globes
Stamped gift tags
Stencilled gift bag
Twiggy wreath

Annie Rigg:
Advent numbered cookies
Apple & cranberry pies
Avocado dip
Bagel chips
Basic vanilla sponge
Bûche de Noel
Buttercream frosting
Candy trees
Cheese & ham scones
Cheese straws
Cheesy grissini
Chocolate brownie squares
Chocolate frosting
Chocolate glaze
Chocolate truffles
Christmas drinks
Cinnamon sticky buns
Coconut ice
Cranberry & pear relish
Cranberry streusel muffins
Cream cheese & herb dip
Easy fruit cake
French toast
Frosted fruit
Frosty the snowman
Gingerbread house
Glacé icing
Iced Christmas tree cookies
Lebkuchen
Marshmallow snowmen
Meringue snowflakes
Mini baked Alaskas
Pain d'épices
Pecan, toffee & chocolate squares
Peppermint creams
Pesto palmiers
Popcorn garlands
Popcorn marshmallow clusters
Pumpkin pie
Red pepper & chickpea dip
Ricciarelli
Sausage rolls
Scotch pancakes with smoked salmon
Shortbread
Snowflake cookies
Spiced nuts
Swedish saffron buns
Toffee apples

Photography credits

Lisa Linder: pages 1, 2, 7 above right, 7 below right, 74–153

Polly Wreford: pages 3, 4–5, 6 above left, 6 below left, 6 below centre, 8–73

Ryland Peters & Small would like to thank all the children that appear as models in this book: Aimee, Alessandra, Alissia, Amelia, Anna, Archie, Ayesha, Bella, Bluebelle, Cameron, Celia, Chantal, Charlie, Constance & Lydia, David, Donnell-Andre, Ella & Ben, Emma & Julian, Hannah, Hassia, Honor, Imani & India, Jack, Jago, Jessica, Kai, Mackie, Malise, Marly, Max & Timmy, Parisa, Polly & Will, Saffron, Saskia, Thomas & Ollie, Tom, Tommy and William.